Praise for
SHOWTIME!!!

SHOWTIME!!! *masterfully reveals how theatrical skills are fundamental to success in business and life. This book is a brilliant read filled with valuable nuggets you cannot afford to miss.*

– JAYNIE SMITH
Best Selling Author of Creating Competitive Advantage
and Relevant Selling

Bernie Cronin cracks the code on excellence—he is a master of his medium.
SHOWTIME!!! *will spur you to unlock your purpose, knowledge, and passion and, as a result, help to transform your life.*

– CHARLIE ANDERSON
President, Selling Skills Institute and Best-Selling Author

To Will
Perform Like a
Champion every day

Bernie

CONTACT BERNIE

To schedule Bernie to speak at your event, call:
(954) 295-9202

For more information, go to:
www.berniecronin.com

SHOWTIME
Mission

The Mission of SHOWTIME is to help readers discover that life, much like the stage, is about plays, shows, acts, scenes, and roles, some personal and some professional, and the key to success in these various endeavors is threefold: Planning, Preparation, and Performance.

Acknowledgements

Charlie Anderson

Barry Cronin

Michael Cronin

Dan Cronin

Daniella Coy

Angel Denker

Mark Graham

Mary Harris

Ken Horkavy

Ken LaVetter

Myles Martel

Jaynie Smith

Joe Stout

Erin Ross

And, of course, my High School Sweetheart and wife, Helen!

FOREWORD

*Ronald Reagan's Personal Debate Advisor and Advisor to
White House Office of Communications*

Dr. Myles Martel, PhD

I met Bernie Cronin more than 10 years ago at an alumni function hosted in Boca Raton, Florida by our alma mater, The University of Connecticut. He made an instant positive impression on me as a smart, upbeat fellow whom I wanted to get to know better. Since then, our personal and professional friendship has grown to a point where I could fill an album teeming with quite a collection of great memories.

Of the many memories I could share that are relevant to this book, one that stands out is when I turned to him to seek his counsel for a seminar I was conducting several years ago for one of my major clients, a Fortune 500 company. Part of the seminar involved "the art of handling objections." Although I had considerable experience teaching "the art of handing difficult questions," and published two books related to this subject, he shared with me insights and techniques regarding handling objections that were eye-opening, enriched my seminar, and enhanced my client's reaction to it.

I expect *Showtime* to be both eye-opening and enriching to you, regardless of your profession or age. Bernie has done a masterful job of gleaning insights from several disciplines, especially theatre, psychology and business. He weaves them into a compelling narrative that can appeal to a broad audience: it can help someone who is working hard to become successful; it can help make someone who is successful — even a star — to become even more successful.

His use of the acting metaphor to give a coherent and eminently practical approach to *Showtime* is inspiring. By focusing on acting, he makes a powerful case for how much we are all engaged in the art of acting, whether we realize it or not. And as he does, he avoids the all-too-fatal trap of producing lists of superficial tips as he makes us more methodically mindful of every critical aspect of our presentation of self.

The importance of being optimistic and radiating optimism, fundamental tenets to success in any walk of life, are well explained throughout *Showtime*. To Bernie's credit, he does not treat optimism as a tip, but as a state of being.

And for anyone who has seen him teach or knows him, he exemplifies this tenet better than most anyone I have ever met. Optimism, as he implies, is the wellspring for confidence, approachability, and ultimately, happiness and success.

Showtime highlights well the significance of storytelling to the process of selling or persuasion. Too many managers and presentation coaches extol the importance of storytelling, yet too few give practical guidance regarding how to shape a good story. Drawing from a breadth of well-grounded teachings and his own impressive background, Bernie lays out a clear method for crafting a clear, engaging, results-oriented narrative that can contribute to his reader's success. In a phrase, impressive stuff!

So many books are, in effect, teasers, where the author cleverly shares only so much so you will buy his next book. The more I think about *Showtime*, the more I regard it as a wonderfully generous contribution—an extraordinary treasure trove of insights, wisdom, and guidance.

May you savor *Showtime*, capitalize on its enormous value, and celebrate the successes that it, combined with your talent and drive, will help you deservedly earn

Sincerely,

Myles Martel,
Ph.D. President and CEO Martel & Associates Gulfstream, Florida

TABLE OF CONTENTS

INTRODUCTION...................................... 1
Let the Show Begin

ACT 1 17
The World of Theater

ACT 2 61
The World of Business

ACT 3 91
Roles of the Actor

ACT 4 113
Roles of the Business Performers

ACT 5 133
Roles of the Producer and Director

ACT 6 151
Roles of the Executive and Manager

ACT 7 173
The Audition

ACT 8 189
The Interview

ACT 9 213
Academy Awards

ENCORE 229
Parallels of Theater and Business

ADDENDUM A..................................... 243
Bernie-isms

ADDENDUM B..................................... 267
Recommended Reading/Listening/Study

ADDENDUM C..................................... 271
National Acting Programs

ADDENDUM D..................................... 275
Bernie's Acting Programs and Testimonials

ADDENDUM E..................................... 281
*Coming Attractions: Bernie's Speaking
and Training Topics*

"Life is a performing art."
BERNIE CRONIN

LET THE SHOW BEGIN

I'm writing this book to help as many readers as possible, in business and life, discover how their worlds of theater, business, and life are all connected and involve commitment, continuous study, and a conscious understanding of what it takes to be a successful lifetime professional, versus a first-year rookie, in whatever their chosen profession. My goal is to weave together art, science, spirituality, psychology, and economics to interlace these three worlds.

So, is business a *Broadway Show* or is acting a *Business Show*? It's probably a question of semantics but if you look at the desired results of both professions, you'll find they both lead their audience to an emotion and a decision based on the credibility of the performance.

As a result of my 40 years in sales, sales management, business ownership, consulting, and speaking, and as a student of acting, I find that business and acting both involve:

- Helping an audience discover your message (Socratic method)

- An opening (curtain), a presentation (scenes), and a close (curtain)

- The audience interacting either consciously or subconsciously

- The performer proving credibility

Whether it's the teachings of Stanislavski, Meisner, Strasberg, or Adler in theater, or Dale Carnegie, Brian Tracy, Tom Hopkins, or Tony Robbins in business, the goals are similar to this book: give the reader a system or methodology for applying their craft in a professional and credible manner.

Think about the ACTS and the SCENES in your daily life:

To live a life of integrity and authenticity is to remain

true to one's self while engaging in socially appropriate roles. Whether we are playing mother, father, wife, teacher, friend, daughter/son, seeker, student, sister, brother or entertainer, there is a common thread that weaves through all of them so that none are ever in conflict with another.

ACT I: EARLY DAY

SCENE 1: You awaken and select your costume, makeup, and hairstyle for the day, based on the audiences you will perform for (when I meet with bankers, I always select my white shirts and conservative suit and tie).

SCENE 2: You proceed to your theater and select your schedule and behaviors to perform as a star in your respective role (student, teacher, leader, manager, customer service agent, receptionist, technician, etc.)

SCENE 3: You stage and cast your meetings and presentations (in person, or via Skype, conference calls, or webinars, and receive and send e-mails and texts and make and receive telephone calls).

INTERMISSION: AT MIDDAY, YOU HAVE AN INTERMISSION.
ACT II: AFTERNOON

SCENE 4: In the afternoon you prepare for your afternoon

performances, ending your first of the day's roles.

SCENE 5: Fitness Center, you again proceed to your dressing room and select your costume (sweat suit for a workout or shorts and shirt for your walk).

ACT III: EVENING

SCENE 6: You arrive home and prepare for the multiple interactions with your spouse, significant other, and extended family.

SCENE 7: After your evening interlude, you proceed to your main stage for your nightly TV performances or Kindle/ Nook/ e-book or Facebook/Facetime with friends and family.

SCENE 8: Later, you again proceed to your dressing room and select your sleeping attire for renewing your energy in order to perform the next day.

Sound familiar? Does this describe, in some respect, the roles you play in a day? Think about the experience your prospective customers and clients have when they enter your office or place of business: What they see (Testimonials, Mission Statement, Pictures, Periodicals, etc.); what they hear (from the receptionist, greeter, background music, or TV blaring); how they feel (welcome, comfortable); what they smell (flowers, scented office); and what they taste (complimentary mints, water, coffee, smoothie!).

Think about what your prospects, customers, and clients *hear* when your staff picks up the phone and greets callers—or are you so blind to reality that you "step over dollars to pick up dimes" (a Bernie-ism) and have an automated, lifeless telephone system that gives nine different alternatives to choose from and sends callers to cyberspace if they

> "No matter how you feel, get up, dress up and show up."
>
> STEVE GILLILAND

don't know someone's extension? If so—get with it. You spend thousands and millions to get the phone to ring

… For what? So your callers get lost in the ether?

Two of the best, and least used, words in the English language are "THANK YOU." I always answer my phone (even when my wife is calling), "Thank you for calling Bernie." I'm happy my phone rings and I don't have to pick it up and make a cold call to a stranger! And my phone message is the same: "THANK YOU for calling Bernie. Please leave a message and I'll call you back as soon as I am able." Short, sweet, courteous, and to the point. I encourage all of my clients to use the same proven phone greeting: "Thank you for calling 'ABC Company.' This is " " How may I help you?"

In 1999, I went to New York to see actor Brian Dennehy play the role of Willie Loman in the 50th anniversary of Arthur

Miller's tragedy *Death of a Salesman*. Willy is the consummate failure driven by fears of rejection and doubts. Leaving the theater with tears in my eyes, I asked myself, "How many millions of wannabe entrepreneurs and business people have suffered from these terrible delusions over the years and how many more will suffer in the future?"

In preparing for this unexpected exploration of how theater, business, and life mirror one another, I have studied theater; owned several successful and unsuccessful businesses; trained thousands of students in leadership and management and lived life to the fullest.

Just look at the parallels that play so importantly into each of these worlds. Whether it's theater, leadership, entrepreneurship, business ownership, or day-to-day living, we audition, perform, improvise, engage, interact, and get a response—either positive or negative— from our audiences. All convey their approval or disapproval of our performance. This can lead to a short and undistinguished run or it can lead to the big time—meaning a long run on Broadway or other forms of success.

I come from a business development background. I'm a personal and business coach by profession. In that world, a long run means a major client who buys from me year after year because of how I perform and not because of price, terms, or conditions—three factors that are always subject to change. For better or worse, the one constant of the man or woman who owns or manages a business or professional service must deliver an experience her audience (customer/client) wants and needs. As Herman Melville wrote, "To produce a mighty book, you must choose a mighty theme. No great and enduring volume can ever be written on the fly, though many there be who have tried it."

I believe *Showtime* represents a mighty theme; it is a theme I've been contemplating for many years,and the results are captured within these pages, much as a play is brought to life within the walls of a theater, big or small.

In the business world, 70 percent of all companies fail within the first three years.

In the real world, 50 percent of all marriages fail. And the percentage is even higher for second and third marriages.

In the world of theater, it is said that at any point in time, 95 percent of all actors are out of work. On the other hand, it is reported that 82% of employees in the field of arts and entertainment reported being satisfied in their field of employment (Source: Monster.com 2014).

What is the underlying basis for these turnover and failure rates? It is the inability of people to connect with others on a personal and emotional level. It is this very lack of connection that makes an actor effective or ineffective.

William Shakespeare said it best when he wrote: "All the

world's a stage, and all the men and women merely players ...
And one man in his time plays many parts."

KEEP PLAYING!!!

THE INSTRUMENT

Eric Morris has been the acting coach for, among
many others, Jack Nicholson, Michelle Pfeiffer, and Johnny
Depp. In his classes, he refers to the actor's persona as the
"INSTRUMENT."

In theater, if the actor cannot be clearly heard or
understood, the audience will quickly lose interest and tune out.
In the worlds of business, leadership, and entrepreneurship, if
the "performer" cannot be clearly heard and understood, his
or her audience will likewise lose interest and tune out.

Cecily Berry says, "Your voice is a very particular
expression of your own personality ... it is the means by which
you convey your thoughts and feelings in an immediate way
to other people." Berry may have been referring to the actor
on stage, but she could just as easily have been talking about a
husband and wife in conversation, a business owner relaying
strategy to his or her team, or a 16-year-old boy asking a girl
out for the first time.

If the business leader, the entrepreneur, or the man (or
woman) on the street wants to convey a message successfully,
then it's important that they embrace the technical aspects

actors use every day on stage: tonality, pace, inflection, cadence, body language, and projection, as well as the creative aspects of speech, movement, and connection.

METHODOLOGIES, SYSTEMS, AND SCHOOLS

According to the dictionary, a methodology is defined as, "A body of practices, procedures, and rules used by those who work in a discipline or engage in an inquiry; a set of working methods."

In the world of theater, we have:

- The Stanislavski Technique

- Delsarte System of Dramatic Expression

- The Vakhtang of School of Stage Art

- Meyerhhold's Biomechanics in Acting

- Viola Spolin and the Theater of Games

- Bertold Brecht and the Theater of Politics

- Jerzy Grotowski and the Holy Actor

- Tadashi Suzuki and the Theater of Grandeur

- Stella Adler

- Strasberg's Method

- The Sanford Meisner Approach

- Eric Morris Method

Lee Strasberg, Stella Adler, and Sanford Meisner all came to their teaching from their work with the Group Theater. They were dedicated to using and extending the Stanislavski/ Vakhtangof System and teaching it to American actors. The Group Theater was formed in 1930 by 27 actors in Danbury, Connecticut. The Group spokesman was Harold Clurman, who'd been giving talks in New York City about a new American theater to anyone who would listen. The Group felt they needed a single vision, and that actors needed a common vocabulary and purpose. Clurman preached that this vision could only be attained by the study and application of the ideas of Constantine Stanislavski. Assisted by Cheryl Crawford and Lee Strasberg, these three would forge the most important and influential theater in America in its time. As a group, they have trained some of the most influential actors and teachers of the late 20th century and are often regarded as the gurus of acting methodology.

Communication requires a process of thought and action. Even if you espouse improvisation when you're conducting a business meeting or asking a girl out on a date, you've still chosen a methodology. Good or bad, it is still a process.

Defenders of certain teachers and methods may cite the great actors who've been trained by those particular teachers.

The truth is that many famous actors have gone to many different teachers and coaches in search of approaches that might help them. For example, Robert Duvall studied with both Sanford Meisner and Lee Strasberg; Marlon Brando studied with Stella Adler and Elia Kazan; and Robert DeNiro studied with both Adler and Strasberg. Adler says, "You cannot play a big play from the words—you have to play it from the conflicts." In Chapter 1, we discuss the Drama Triangle of Persecutor > Victim > Rescuer in what is the essence of conflict. Not just on stage, but also in the boardroom, on the factory floor and the schoolyard, in the field of battle, and the football field. Conflict is where growth comes from. It's where change comes from.

I have studied with Eric Morris, Frank Licari, and the Burt Reynolds Institute of Film & Theater (BRIFT) in Jupiter, Florida, where I enrolled in the Emerging Playwrights Program, lived the acting life for a time, and met a wonderful group of creative people.

I think we should all ask ourselves who our mentors are. Who have we studied under? Who has made the greatest impression on us? What methodologies do we use in our professions? If we can identify the methodologies and techniques that we use in our professional and personal lives, then we have a set of tools we can adapt to fit just about any situation.

In business there are many useful systems and

methodologies. Among them we have:

- Accounting Systems

- Auditing Systems

- Compliance Systems

- Hiring Systems

- Inventory Systems

- Marketing Systems

- Pricing Systems

- Procurement Systems

Whatever system you choose, whether it's related to the business world, your everyday life, or the theater, you essentially give yourself a MapQuest for conveying your message or messages consistently, exactly as the actor does on stage night after night.

Here, I'd like to give special credit to Dale Carnegie, the father of self-improvement and personal development as we know it today. Carnegie was born in 1888 in Missouri and was educated at Warrensburg State Teachers College. As a salesman and aspiring actor, he traveled to New York and began teaching communications classes to adults at the YMCA. In 1912, the world famous Dale Carnegie Course© was born.

He authored several bestsellers, including the first mass-market public-speaking and self-help book, *The Art of Public Speaking*, in 1915, followed by *How to Win Friends and Influence People* and *How to Stop Worrying and Start Living*. In *The Art of Public Speaking*, he said stories were powerful ways of connecting emotionally with your audience, and three-quarters of a century before PowerPoint was invented, Carnegie was talking about using visual aids. He was a prominent lecturer and a sought-after counselor to world leaders. His legacy today is a worldwide network of more than 2,700 trainers with offices in more than 85 countries.

EMOTIONS

There is one thing that these various approaches have in common, whether we're talking about an acting system, a business methodology, or a life practice—and that is their focus on emotions.

Here's an age-old metaphor that I use to illustrate this point: "If information could change behavior, no one would smoke." Success in business and life, just like acting, comes from making an emotional connection with your audience, and you can boost your leadership   effectiveness, as well as your personal relationships at home and work, by having a clear understanding of the power of emotion.

I love the quote by Dr. Edward Hallowell, author of *Shine*, when he says, "Communication is sharing information;

connecting is sharing emotions." Now that's a life philosophy that works in the theater, the business world, and at home. Hallowell is a Harvard professor and author of the bestselling book on Attention Deficit Disorder (ADD), titled *Driven to Distraction*.

EMOTION MEMORY

In the world of theater, Constantine Stanislavsky's most controversial technique is called Emotion Memory. The promise of his system is that if you use imagination to enter, with belief, the imaginary circumstances of the play, and if you follow the correct objectives and actions through the play's length, then the proper emotions will follow you and inspiration will more than likely manifest itself.

> "We don't think ourselves into a new way of acting; we ACT ourselves into a new way of thinking."
>
> BERNIE CRONIN

In the year 1900, a book called *The Psychology of the Emotions* by French psychologist Theodore Ribot was translated into Russian. As the story goes, Stanislavsky read it and was greatly influenced by it. Ribot stated that all life experiences are recorded in the nervous system. To Stanislavsky, this meant the actor could call up emotions from his past and apply them to the emotional life of the character. Under the proper circumstances, emotions were the tricky part, and to call up his emotions, Stanislavsky taught the technique known as Sense Memory. For example, if your character were to cry in a certain scene, you were taught to recall how you felt in the past when you cried in a certain situation and apply it to your character and the present circumstances of the scene. In current-day psychology, it's called Reachback. In other words, you reach back into your past and recapture the emotions.

While Stanislavsky was talking primarily about the world of theater, he was making an amazing point about everyday life and leadership as well. We often use our memories to guide our actions and our responses, and this is not a behavioral trait we want to fight. It's a tool we want to study and embrace.

IT'S NOT THE WORDS, IT'S THE CONFLICT

The book *Stella Adler on America's Master Playwrights* makes it clear that Stella Adler rarely lectured about text or the use of words.

Rather, it's all about subtext—the writer's background, emotional life, spiritual needs, and everything that goes into the structure of the words.

Adler had a number of students who went on to great

acclaim, most prominently Marlon Brando, who always swore that he learned more from her than any other teacher.

Unless she was working on a specific scene with her actors, Adler never talked about the moment-to-moment of a scene, but rather the underpinning of what the author was trying to communicate. In other words, what is the emotion behind it all?

Melding the theater with business and life also begins with an understanding of the underpinnings of emotion. More important, it is about communicating this emotion and using it to your advantage. It is this emotion that draws us to the characters on stage. It is the emotion that motivates our employees and lets us see into the hearts of our clients and customers. And it is this emotion that makes our personal relationships worth treasuring.

So with that, enjoy a *Weekend with Bernie* and "Let the Show Begin!"

"All the world's a stage and all the men and women are merely players. They have their exits and entrances; each man in his time plays many parts."

WILLIAM SHAKESPEARE

ACT ONE

THE WORLD OF THEATER

PLAYBILL

In Act 1, The World of Theater, we will explore the many aspects of the theater, from the playwright and the audition, to the hundreds of hours of rehearsal time and the energy and jitters of opening night. We will explore how this wonderful world comes together and, in so many ways, emulates the life we lead—how it relates to your role in the business world and your day-to-day life, and how it speaks to your role as a leader, a business person, a spouse, a parent, and a friend to the world.

DISCOVER

- Why the art of storytelling is fundamental to theater

- How theater and the fabric of life come together

- How actors are made, not born

- How the drama and business triangles intersect

LET THE SHOW BEGIN

The beginning of theater dates back to the onset of civilization. It was initially a form of storytelling, and, well, it still is. Cognitive scientist Mark Turner calls storytelling "narrative imaging," a key instrument of thought.

We are all wired to tell and receive stories. We are all born "storytellers" and "story-listeners." As kids, we looked forward to "Show and Tell." We gathered with our friends at recess or lunchtime and told stories about real things and real events that mattered; at least, they mattered to us! Acting is a normal human activity. Everybody acts in one way or another almost every day. Acting is a way of showing our understanding of the world and passing it on to other people.

"God made man because he loves stories," wrote Elie Wiesel, a Holocaust survivor and Nobel Laureate. Wiesel authored *Night*, his bestselling memoir about his experience with his father in the Nazi concentration camps at Auschwitz and Buchenwald in 1944–1945. Everyone in his family perished except Elie. I particularly like this quote because of its implication that stories and parables are how God first communicated with us. The Old Testament is filled with stories, from tragedies to triumphs. Six thousand years ago, most ancient people were illiterate. They learned about God from stories that were passed down from one generation to the next.

When I was young, we had Walt Disney, founder of Disneyland and master storyteller and animator, who once said, "Animation offers a medium of storytelling and visual entertainment which can bring pleasure and information to people of all ages everywhere in the world." He had that right!

The art of storytelling recently received a boost from the world of marketing in an article written for the trade magazine, *AdWeek,* by John Hamm, Chief Creative and Innovative Officer at Momentum Worldwide (I love his title). Hamm describes the difference between branded content and true storytelling this way:

"Stories rely on the intended audience to develop their own imagery and detail to complete and, most importantly, to co-create, whereas content does not. The truly great storytellers have long embraced the fact that the most powerful stories happen in the mind of the audience, making each and every story unique and personal for the individual. Stories are how we pass on our accumulated wisdom, beliefs, and values. They are the process through which we describe and explain the world around us, and our role and purpose in it. Audiences have always known this and asked for stories—they've never asked for content."

Mr. Hamm has hit it right on the head. If you want to truly influence another person, tell them a story. Drop them right into a scene filled with drama and dialogue and changing images. Allow them to fill in the blanks. Make them a part of the story.

Suddenly, they begin to take ownership of an idea, and it becomes their own, something to act upon and be a part of. This isn't just the theater we're talking about here. This works for the boardroom and the manufacturing floor. It works for a call. It works for a quiet dinner between two young lovers or the oldest married couple.

As I like to say, "The power is in the story. Long live the art of storytelling."

Storytelling is the heart of drama. No two people tell a story the same way. In the same vein, good leaders are, in essence, good storytellers, because they have the ability to not only describe their purpose but also to give direction and motivation to achieve that purpose. That's what makes the melding of theater, business, and life so compelling and so obvious.

The TV show *"Dancing with the Stars"* judge Carrie Ann Inaba, who grew up in Honolulu, says she got her start in dancing with the hula. "It's a form of storytelling; it's almost a language," she said.

People can relate to a good story well told, because it gives them the opportunity to learn and grow and change.

Aristotle once said, "A good story has a beginning, a middle, and an end." It sounds obvious to us now, but that one solid idea has lived with us for thousands of years and continues to be a major influence in the arts today. Life isn't all that different. There is a beginning, middle, and end, and no part is less important than another.

Authors Muriel James and Dorothy Jongeward in their bestseller *Born to Win*, about the psychological movement Transactional Analysis, discuss "LIFE SCRIPTS," the plans you consciously or unconsciously have for how you are going to live your life. They wrote "Life is often like a play, and humans will adopt roles based on what they have been told about themselves by their family or culture. "We begin life," the authors said, "as slaves to our parents, but some people remain so all of their lives. Whether we like it or not, we are given a story to act out that may or may not suit us, and the mature human being will feel the need, at some point, to shake off their script like a skin and write their own story."... WOW!!!

WHAT IS THEATER?

Theater is the branch of the performing arts defined by Bernard Beckerman this way: "Theater occurs when one or more persons, isolated in time and space, present themselves to another or others."

By this broad definition, theater has existed since the dawn of man, as a result of the human tendency toward *storytelling*. Since its inception, theater has come to take on many forms, utilizing speech, gestures, costumes, music, dance, and spectacle, while combining other performing and visual arts into a single artistic form. The word derives from the ancient Greek *theatron*, meaning "the seeing place." Theater involves more than just the actors. It involves writers, producers, directors, music composers, singers, dancers, comedians, tragedians, choreographers, costume makers, make-up artists, stagehands, prop guys, and supernumeraries. Did I get you with that one? Supernumeraries are extras in the cast with no speaking roles who are called simply "Supers."

HISTORY AND STORYTELLING

On a *60 Minutes* program in November 2012, Morley Safer asked historian and author David McCulloch to explain the most important part of relating history, as he'd done with books on US presidents George Washington, John Adams, and Harry Truman.

"The key to researching and writing a historical

biography is storytelling. It's taking events and facts and personalities and weaving them into a story," said McCulloch.

He notes that American politics has always been rough and ready. "Thomas Jefferson and John Adams went at each other with fire tongs." He gives the second and third US presidents lots of credit, but when asked to name the greatest president of them all, this is what he said, "George Washington was the greatest. He had no examples to go by. He did everything right. I wish I could have been there." "And here's what's impressive about Washington from my point of view," he continued. "He wasn't playing just one role. He was the face of a nation, a leader of men, a businessman, and a family man, and he performed each and every one like a Broadway headliner."

Speaking of presidents, Ronald Reagan, the 44th US president, had three predominant interests in his life: Sports, Drama, and Politics.

Reagan attended tiny Eureka College in Illinois and was a member of the Eureka Players; Eureka didn't have a drama department per se, so the Players had to improvise. During Reagan's sophomore year, the Players participated in the 5th

> # "Life isn't about finding yourself. Life is about creating yourself."
>
> ## GEORGE BERNARD SHAW

Annual Theater Tournament at Northwestern University and were awarded third place among nine competing groups. Reagan was named among the six best actors of the tournament. Perhaps more importantly, he was encouraged by some very influential theater people to pursue a career in acting, and we all know how successful that decision turned out to be: star of movies and television, and president of the Screen Actors Guild.

Reagan was an avid moviegoer. As a child, he experienced the advent of talking pictures. He was particularly swept away by westerns and the vivid use of a Persecutor, a Victim, and a Rescuer.

Perhaps what's most interesting to me about Ronald Reagan was the comment he made when asked about what his plans were for a prospective career after college: "I have no definite plans for the future other than trying to get a position in some business, probably as a salesman." And a salesman he was: he sold himself to Hollywood as an actor, the populace of California as governor, and the voting majority of the United States as president in 1980 and again in 1984.

I love when I get together with my friend and fellow University of Connecticut Alumnus, Dr. Myles Martel, who was Pres. Reagan's Speech and Debate Advisor and Director of White House Communications during Reagan's first term. His stories of Reagan's preparation and commitment give credence to why he was called "THE

GREAT COMMUNICATOR". In 2011, on what would have been Reagan's 100th Birthday, Myles and I hosted a Reagan Birthday party at my club and Myles delivered his program *"The Leadership Legacies of Ronald Reagan"*....a smash performance. In addition he offered a display of his collection of mementos from every president from George Washington to Barack Obama. Of course I had to hire a security officer to guard the collection.

In a 2012 interview, Doris Kearns Goodwin, the author of the 2006 best-selling book *Team of Rivals: The Political Genius of Abraham Lincoln*, said, "So many people just see that face [Lincoln's face] that looks so sad, but when he told a story, his whole face would light up and change." She said, "People of that era often wrote about how irritated they would get because Lincoln was telling stories all the time, but that was Lincoln." He once remarked in a brief story of humility, "I do generally remember a good story when I hear it, but I never did invent anything original; I am only a retail dealer."

The structure for storytelling developed in the 19th century when German playwright Gustav Freytag developed his seven- step "Freytag's Pyramid":

1. EXPOSITION: the background, setting, characters, setting the scene

2. INCITING INCIDENT: something happens to begin the action

3. RISING ACTION: the story builds

4. CLIMAX: the point of greatest tension

5. FALLING ACTION: events that happen as a result of the climax

6. RESOLUTION: the character solves the problem/conflict

7. DENOUEMENT: French term meaning the ending

My point here is that storytelling has been around since the beginning of time. It is a vehicle that you and I both use, whether we are selling a product to a customer or telling our kids a bedtime story. The better we are at it, the more effective we are.

READING, WRITING, AND STORYTELLING

In a 2012 *New York Times* interview, Dennis Lehane, author of *Live by Night*, *Gone Baby Gone*, and *Mystic River*, was asked, "If you could give one piece of advice to aspiring novelists, what would it be?"

Lehane responded by saying, I believe so deeply in the primacy of language, of lifting your prose to the highest level you're capable of and making your words symphonic. But I worry that writing programs spend too much time on the words and not enough on the story. Faulkner understood story, but he had such astounding technical skill he could seem to abandon it and no one would care. But most students don't have that staggering degree of technical ability, so they should learn to tell a story first. That's what it is at the end of the day: storytelling. So my best piece of advice to aspiring novelists— after READ and read some more—would be: Don't think of yourselves as writers; think of yourselves as storytellers.

Whether you're writing copy for your blog, delivering a talk to your industry association, introducing yourself at a networking function, talking to prospective clients at a trade show, pitching your novel or screenplay, writing articles or web copy, creating an ad or commercial, interviewing for a job or competing for a contract at a bid meeting you're not finished until you've shared a story with human interaction. When is your next communication event? Use these three steps to make your message even more impactful to your audience:

Step 1. Identify a story that shares an epiphany that is relevant to your audience and congruent with the purpose of your communication

Step 2. Who are the "Cast of Characters"? Identify at least two people who were involved in the situation. Describe the scene so readers or listeners can see and visualize them in their minds.

Step 3. Map out what each player actually said. Capture the actual words and underlying emotion that was present at the time so that your audience is right there with you in the moment.

TED TALKS—STORIES ILLUMINATE, INFORM, AND INSPIRE

Bryan Stevenson, a civil rights attorney who wins cases in front of the US Supreme Court, gave a TED Talk in 2012 and received the longest standing ovation in TED history. In 18 minutes, Stevenson told three personal stories reinforcing his theme that in poor communities, many people grow up without a sense of identity and make profoundly harmful decisions as a result. Stories made up 65 percent of Stevenson's content. The statistics Stevenson used to back his arguments comprised only 25 percent of his presentation (the rest fell under the category of "ethos," establishing credibility). Statistics support your argument but stories connect you with your audience.

PACKAGING THE MESSAGE IN AN UNEXPECTED WAY

In 2009, Bill Gates gave a TED talk on reducing childhood deaths in Africa. "Malaria is spread by mosquitoes," Gates told the audience as he picked up a glass jar sitting on a table in front of him. He opened the jar and said, "I brought some here. I'll let them roam around. There is no reason only poor people should be infected."

The audience sat in stunned silence for a moment, then laughed, applauded, and cheered. They weren't happy about the topic, of course, but they knew that Gates had given them a novel way to consider the problem. Gates had created what neuroscientists call an "emotionally charged event." It's a shocking, impressive, or surprising moment that is so moving and memorable that it grabs the listener's attention and is remembered long after the presentation is over.

Emille Gruppe, a prominent artist in my adopted hometown of Gloucester, Massachusetts, once said, "Painting is like storytelling. No two people tell a story the same way. That's what makes art so interesting."

And I say: That's what makes life so interesting. No two people look at the world exactly the same way. We need to embrace this uniqueness, just as the actor embraces their unique view of the characters they are portraying. Make life, and your roles in it, your own.

In April 2013, I attended a Kenny Rogers concert at the Kravis Center in West Palm Beach, Florida. Kenny's brother Randy is a good friend of mine. He was employed as an event coordinator and community outreach advisor for one of my longtime Fort Lauderdale clients, Mahoney & Associates. In a storied career of nearly five-and-a-half decades, Kenny has endeared music lovers around the globe with his amazing songs, heartfelt performances, and rare storytelling ability.

Kenny once told *Billboard Magazine*, "I've never considered myself a great singer, but I am a great storyteller."

In 2005, my wife and I were having dinner with friends at a Palm Beach restaurant called BICE, and there was a group of seven older ladies seated near us. They were having dinner and celebrating one of their group's birthday. At the end of dinner, the waiter appeared with the pre-arranged cake, and the staff sang the traditional "Happy Birthday." Unbeknownst to anyone in the group, Kenny Rogers happened to be having dinner in a quiet corner with friends, and, like all of us, was aware of the celebration. Wanting to add to the festivities, Kenny approached the women, said happy birthday to the birthday girl, and proceeded to sing "Happy Birthday" to her in that unmistakable voice of his. If only I'd had a camera and could have captured the look on her surprised face. What a class act!

When I told that story to Kenny's brother Randy, he shrugged his shoulders and said, "Oh, that's just Kenny being Kenny."

I thought of it a little differently. Kenny was on stage, even though it wasn't the typical performing stage we all picture. It is much like a CEO playing golf with his peers on a Tuesday afternoon. He may not be in his office or the boardroom, but you had better believe that he is in full CEO mode and performing just like he would if it was at the office.

The truth is, we're all players; sometimes the stage changes and we have to improvise, but we're still players and that's why we call it a *PLAYGROUND* not a DO GROUND!!!

QUOTATIONS

Think of quotations as "verbal shorthand." They condense complicated concepts into an accessible language nugget. Even more importantly these pearls of wisdom can inspire people to shift and change their ways because they point out precedence and credibility, and how others have adopted a constructive behavior or belief. They help people learn from the successes and failures of others. I have over 500 quotations in my writing and speaking arsenal and often condense them down into specific topics like theater, beliefs, failures, successes and life.

TRANSFORMATION

In Greece, sometime around 534 BC, the first professional actor on record, a man known as Thespis of Icaria, took the stage in the role of a tragic hero. Thus, the name we use to describe actors is "Thespians." Back then, the story was delivered in the third person. "He walked down the road..." It was more telling than showing. These days, the actors' job is to transform themselves into the role, dropping the character right into whatever scene the playwright has created, and taking the audience right along with them. We call this *transformation*, and we all do it. We transform to fit wherever the setting—or scene—might be. We act differently at a cocktail party than we do when sitting at home watching television with our spouse. The CEO acts differently in a strategy session than he does with a fishing rod in his hand on a river in Colorado. The teenager acts differently with his buddies than he does over an ice cream sundae with his girlfriend.

DEATH OF A SALESMAN

In 1949, Lee J. Cobb and Mildred Dunnock co-starred in the Tony-winning Broadway production of Arthur Miller's *Death of a Salesman*. Cobb played the "failure salesman" Willy Loman, an American dreamer fighting a losing battle with fortune and success and fears and doubts.

In an essay written for *The New York Times* on the first anniversary of the play, Miller called Willy "a man who believed he was alone. A man who didn't meet the qualifications laid down by those clean-shaven frontiersmen who inhabit the peaks of broadcasting and advertising offices."

Hearing the "thundering command to succeed," Willy found himself with no recourse but to "stare in the mirror at a failure."

There are surely many men and women today who, like Willy, believe that their inability to achieve the golden ideal of financial success is somehow a personal indictment. As I coach, I tell my clients, "It's who you are that's important; not what you have become. If your self-esteem—how you feel about yourself— is at a 10, then your performance will rise to a 10 as well."

The Great Depression, highlighted by the 1929 Stock

Market Crash, was the formative event in Arthur Miller's young life. In a 1958 speech that was later printed in *Harpers Magazine*, he called the Great Depression, "the ground upon which I learned to stand." Born in 1915, he was the son of first-generation immigrants.

His father became a successful manufacturer of women's coats. During Miller's early years, the family lived in splendor. But Miller's father had invested so much money in the Stock Market that the crash pushed the family into comparative poverty, and they were forced to move from their plush townhouse to a small house in Brooklyn.

> # "The only thing you've got in this world is what you can sell. And the funny thing is, you're a salesman, and you don't even know it."
>
> ARTHUR MILLER

I, too, am a child of first-generation Irish immigrants, my father from Killarney and my mother from Galway. They met and married in Worcester, Massachusetts.

NEED FOR APPROVAL

For me, the defining message in *Death of a Salesman* comes

when Willy exults to his son Biff with the classic line: "Biff, my boy, it's important to be well liked."

Not just "liked," but "well liked."

Once again, the playwright uses a quantitative measure to establish a human being's inherent value. I call this: NEED FOR APPROVAL. And I believe it is one of the biggest reasons people fail in this world, and not just in the theater, but in business and life as well.

I know for certain that the need for approval is one of the biggest reasons people fail in my area of expertise: business. People who have a high "need for approval," or to be "well liked," as Willy put it, are (a) acutely allergic to NO, (b) can't handle rejection, and (c) can't ask the tough, timely question.

In interviewing candidates for my clients, I dig deeply for this weakness and often ask, "How important is it to be well liked?" If someone says, "It's important to be liked but more important to be trusted and respected," then I know I'm onto someone good.

Need for approval isn't just the doom of the business person: it also plays a huge role in why leaders fail. Remember, it's not about being right—it is about getting the job done and respecting your vision. The same thing happens in personal relationships. Your need for approval sometimes pushes you into places that aren't healthy and that aren't really in your best interests.

The distinction is this: I may *want* people to like me, but I don't *need* them to like me. It's far more important that they respect me for who I am. I don't need to be liked. I want it. If they choose not to like me, it's their business. And the truth is, not everyone is going to like me.

I have a saying: "How you feel about me is none of my business."

TO LIKE OR NOT TO LIKE

Thanks to the explosion in social media, being "well liked" has become practically a profession in itself. Adults, as well as teenagers, keep assiduous count of their Facebook friends, their LinkedIn connections, and their Twitter followers, measuring their worth by the rise or fall of those numbers. People are turning themselves into products, both for profit and for pleasure, and the inevitable temptation is to equate the popularity of your brand with your fundamental self-worth.

The new call to action is: "LIKE ME" on Facebook. If Willy Loman were alive today, he would probably say: "LIKE ME WELL" on Facebook!

Many of us are willingly becoming versions of Willy Loman, forever on the road—that is, online—selling ourselves and advertising our lifestyles: describing the meal we just had at a fancy restaurant (with uploaded photographs, of course), or the trip we're planning next week or next year. Personally, I don't give a damn, but I do understand and accept the need to be "well liked." Do I think it is in your best interest or mine? No.

Despite Willy Loman's delusions and moral evasion, Miller always insisted on the nobility in his struggle. "The play is really about mortality and leaving something behind," Miller once said. "Willy Loman is trying to write his name on a cake of ice on a hot July day."

Willy Loman's contradictions and failings are all too human and all too common, which is why the hallucinatory last day of his life will always retain the power to command not just our pity but our respect, too.

PREPARATION AND PRACTICE

Constantine Stanislavski was once asked how long it took to effectively learn his system and he said, "It takes two years of training, hard work, and preparation for the actor to get all the parts of my system in place."

The first year he called: Work on the Self. The second year he called: Work on the Role.

In his book *Building a Character*, Stanislavski writes, "An Actor must work all his life, cultivate his mind, train his talents systematically, and develop his character; he may never despair and never relinquish this main purpose—to love his art with all his strength and love it unselfishly."

Shawn Levy, in his book *Paul Newman: A Life*, writes, "Newman worked hard to develop his skills, then worked equally hard to get the most out of the gift he had."

Levy compares Newman to Burt Lancaster. He writes, "Lancaster was another very handsome man untouched by genius, but who worked and worked and worked and worked some more until he became the very best actor he could be."

Eric Morris once told me that the greatest "preparer" he ever coached was Jack Nicholson—again, a man who demonstrated the willingness and strength to work and prepare until he became one with his character.

Just think if we could put that same unselfish love and strength into every relationship we have. Talk about a life changer. John Wooden, the legendary basketball coach at UCLA, reinforced this when he said, "The ability to execute is important, but more important is the willingness to prepare."

Author Doris Kearns Goodwin, whose book was the basis for Steven Spielberg's movie on Abraham Lincoln, gave actor Daniel Day Lewis a tour through Lincoln's home and law office and the Abraham Lincoln Presidential Library and Museum, and said afterwards, "I could tell even then he'd be incredible. He just absorbed it so fully. And afterward he kept reading more about Lincoln. When it comes to preparation, he's on another planet compared to other actors."

And while we're on the subject of Lincoln and preparation, let's look at the preparation of Lincoln's killer, John Wilkes Booth. Just three days after General Robert E. Lee surrendered and the day after Lincoln's final speech, Booth began crafting his plan. Remember, he was born and raised in an acting household. All of his preparation was designed to make him a star producer, director,and choreographer in his biggest performance ever, a presidential assassination that would guarantee his legacy forever. He planned and prepared to shoot the president in a theater where he felt comfortable and knew he would have an audience. He had performed at several theaters in Washington, where he knew every entrance, exit, and hallway. He found out when Lincoln would be attending the theater and which show was being performed so that he could select the right moment in the show for his execution scene, a moment with few actors on stage. Why? So that when he stopped to deliver his immortal line, he would essentially be unchallenged. And while his escape plans were fuzzy, it is understood his plan was to gallop out of Washington and disappear into the south to be with friends and allies. What a preparer!

Speaking of preparation, the work that Harrison Ford put in for his role as Branch Rickey in the 2013 movie *42* is another intense example. Ford had plenty of experience playing fictional icons—Indiana Jones and Han Solo, just to name two—but not much when it came to flesh-and-blood historical figures.

Branch Rickey was the General Manager of the Brooklyn Dodgers, and the man credited with plucking Jackie Robinson from the Kansas City Monarchs, one of the stalwart teams of the Negro Leagues, and making him the first black man to play in the majors.

Ford said he didn't know much about baseball when he agreed to play Rickey—a part he had to lobby for but he knew a great role when he saw one on paper.

Ford knew he could play the gruff, cigar-chewing, church-going Rickey. He knew he could employ extra padding and prosthetics to transform his appearance. But what he had to do was convince writer/director Brian Helgeland that he was the right actor for the part.

In the world of business, I coach my clients in the Socratic Method of Discovery. I want them to understand that we are never in the process of convincing or persuading. It's more about having the prospective client discover that we are the right choice and that our product or service is the right solution for them.

TALENT IS OVERRATED

Geoff Colvin, Business Editor for *Fortune* magazine, spends considerable time in his book *Talent Is Overrated* talking about the hard work and practice that the super performers in sports, music, theater, chess, and such put into their craft.

He differentiates practice from what he calls "Deliberate Practice." Perhaps the best example Colvin gives us of this very conscious approach to practice is Jerry Rice, the Hall of Fame wide receiver for the San Francisco 49ers. Rice's motto was: "Today I will do what others won't do, so tomorrow I can accomplish what others can't."

In his induction into the Pro Football Hall of Fame in 2010, Rice said, "I was afraid to fail. The fear of failure is the engine that has driven me my entire life." In contrast, he also said, "My single regret about my career is I never took the time to enjoy it; I was always working."

Once we've thoroughly prepared and practiced, then we are ready to transform into whatever role we are playing: it could be a character on stage, an entrepreneur making his pitch, or someone raising a child. This notion of transformation—whether we're talking about theater, business, or parenting—is magical. The great power of the actor to become someone else is mesmerizing, just like a CEO stepping away from his role as a dad and walking into a meeting with his team.

A FACE TO MEET THE FACES

I've always been fascinated with Halloween and the lengths people will take to transform into whatever role they have chosen for that night.

At my club, Delray Dunes Golf & Country Club, in Florida,

we always have a Texas Barbecue Night and everyone, including me, dresses up in their wildest cowboy hats, blue jeans, boots, and big belts, transforming into Garth Brooks or Dolly Parton or some facsimile of a country western star, all

for a night of drinking, eating, and ho-downing! All for a night of transformation!

Actors, directors, producers, and psychologists have long made a study of this phenomenon we call transformation, and here are the questions every actor must ask before taking the stage:

- What is acting and how is it done?

- How does someone become someone else?

- Can someone become someone else?

- How much of what an actor does is due to talent?

- Does an actor lose himself/herself in a character, or are the actor and role separate?

- How does the actor deal with his/her emotions?

- How is acting different from real life?

- Does an actor act from "outside in" or "inside out?"

- Is acting an art or a craft?

- How does an actor/actress perform night after night in the same role with the same emotions and enthusiasm?

- What type of training does an actor need?

- Can acting be taught?

Whatever the historical changes in performance methodologies, conventions and conditions, we can say that the four fundamental conditions of a theatrical event are:

1. An Actor

2. An Action

3. A Space

4. A Spectator

PRESENTATIONAL VS. REPRESENTATIONAL

For centuries, the great argument in acting has centered on Presentational versus Representational styles. Or, in other words, should the actor present the character to his or her audience or, as Eric Morris teaches, become the character? Eric refers to this as *"Experiential Acting"* which means the audience is experiencing what the actor is experiencing.

Interestingly, I find myself approaching my relationships in general this way. The more I can empathize with a person— whether it's a family member, friend, or colleague—the more effectively I can get inside their heads and their hearts, and the better I can know them. Some people prefer more distance and more objectivity in their relationships, and such behavior leans more toward the presentational approach. The key is recognizing the style that works best for you and them and making the most of it.

In general, actors choose from a system or methodology that works each style—it might be Drama School training or private study with the Lee Strasberg Method—and that choice will influence their comfort level with presentational acting or representational acting. Again, the key is knowing one from the other and embracing it.

The business person/entrepreneur/professional is likewise left with a similar menu of choices—from Dale Carnegie and Spin Selling to Miller Heiman, or Value Selling—and an appropriate choice between presenting and representing is almost certain to emerge.

Most of the important teachers of theater, business, or life psychology have themselves been actors or business people who have moved beyond the old ways of left-brain thinking. Now, we commonly use our "right brains" to create new methods and techniques; the key word here being *create*.

When I was studying at the Burt Reynolds Institute For Film and Theater, he had as many as 50-plus questions that he would ask his acting students, and each was meant to influence our character preparation. They ranged anywhere from "What type of birth did you have?" and "How do you feel about your mother?" to "Do you gamble?" and "What part of your body do you like least of all?" While these very interesting and sometimes odd questions influenced how you practiced for your particular role, they were also meant to gain insight into your character and the other characters in your play and to instill a sense of empathy for them.

Knowing yourself as well as you possibly can and being comfortable with the person you are affects every interaction you have, whether it's at home, in the community, or in the workplace. That's what Burt Reynolds was trying to say: Look at life from every angle and know yourself better than you ever thought you could.

WHAT MAKES A GREAT ACTOR?

Eric Morris, the actor and acting coach for the likes of Jack Nicholson, Michelle Pfeiffer, and Johnny Depp, likes to say that 95 percent of great acting is preparation. I like to say that 95 percent of success is also preparation.

But what about life and living? Aristotle would say, "You have to have a plan and you have to examine your plan regularly to live a full life." In other words, it's a piece from the same puzzle. You have to prepare if you want to live fully. And if you want to be the CEO of your own company, you'd better be an expert at preparation too.

Over lunch one day, Eric Morris told me that Jack Nicholson was the greatest preparer he'd ever coached. And just look at the acclaim he's had.

It was said that Dustin Hoffman, famous for his portrayal of the autistic Raymond in *Rain Man*, "became" his character with such intensity that he was still "autistic" two months after the movie was shot.

JOHN WAYNE

Born Marion Morrison in 1907, John Wayne dominated the American Cinema for more than four decades, and with 162 feature films from 1949 through 1974, he was one of the top box office stars. Thirty-five years after his death of cancer at 72 in 1979, he still makes the list of top five all-time favorite actors. In his 2014 book *John Wayne: The Life and Legend*, Scott Eyman writes, "We all think we know John Wayne because he seemed to be playing himself in movie after movie." Yet, as Eyman carefully points out, "John Wayne was an invention, a person created layer by layer by an ambitious young actor. Wayne did not write his parts, but he invented the players who played them." "That guy you saw on the screen wasn't really me," Wayne once said. "I'm Duke Morrison, and I never was and never will be a film personality like John Wayne. I know him well. I'm one of his closest students. I have to be. I make a living out of him."

IMPROVISATION (IMPROV)

The *New Oxford American Dictionary* defines the word "play," as it relates to theater, as "representing a character in a theatrical performance or on film." It defines the word "play," as it relates to baseball, football, golf, basketball, hockey, or rugby as: "to engage in a game, activity, or pastime."

We don't say we're "doing" baseball, football, golf, basketball, hockey, or rugby. We say we're "playing" them.

Many of my golfing cronies would probably characterize my approach to the game of golf as "playing" because of my high handicap. And you know? I can live with that.

Improvisation is one of the truest forms of play. The dictionary defines "improvise" this way: "to create and perform (music, drama or verse) spontaneously or without preparation."

We improvise every day. Every one of us. We have to. Life is not laid out for us in a perfect pattern with perfect outcomes. We have to go with the flow sometimes. And sometimes we have to go against the flow and swim upstream. Changing things up usually adds up to results. Thinking on your feet is one of the most important problem-solving devices known to mankind. In the theater, improv was probably initiated at Hull House in Chicago by a woman named Neva Boyd, who used impromptu games to inspire the children of that city's poorer population. She discovered that play brought out these children's expressive potential and brightened their spirits. She soon saw that fun and creativity gave to them what their daily world often denied them: a bold sense of joy!

Viola Spolin, a Stanislavski disciple and teacher, worked with Neva Boyd and helped to develop her ideas further. Spolin created what she called, "Theater Games," first for children and then for adults. She saw that the Stanislavski System, as it was being taught at the time in the United States, often restricted actors in over thinking and seriousness. The sense of playfulness, of "play" itself, was being lost. She realized that playing games was something grown-ups had stopped doing. So, with a group of Chicago actors, she began to explore the possibility of "play" with adult actors centered on improvising characters, speeches, and scenes. In 1963, she wrote a book called *Improvisation for the Theater* that encapsulated these exercises and quickly became a mainstay of theater programs everywhere.

I'm not sure if anyone has ever written a book called *Improvisation for the Boardroom or the Factory Floor*, but it would make for good reading. The best leaders know when to go off script. They know how to motivate with their actions and with their words, and sometimes the most effective leadership they demonstrate is walking among the troops, lending a helping hand, and simply talking off the cuff.

I have embraced the concept of improvisation in my Leadership Coaching with a program I call "Improv and Role-

Play Scenes." I partnered up with actor and teacher Frank Licari, owner of the Atlantic Arts Theater in Jupiter, Florida, and an early member of one of today's great improv groups, Blue Man Group, in developing the program. Our fundamental concept was to show men and women how a touch of improvisation can improve their ability to understand a potential prospect's needs and to generate the kind of empathy that leads to long-term relationships.

Blue Man Group was born in 1988 in New York City when three young guys—an acting student, a magazine researcher, and a software producer—were so happy to see the end of the 1980s that they held a funeral for the decade. They painted their faces blue and led a procession through Central Park; they burned a Rambo doll and a piece of the Berlin Wall. Although they couldn't have known it, Chris Wink, Phil Stanton, and Matt Goldman had launched what would grow into an entertainment juggernaut. Since opening in New York City's Astor Place Theater in 1991, the Blue Man Group has played in 12 cities across the globe. More than 17 million people have seen its shows and today tickets go for $43 to $132. Founder Goldman said "The whole show is about connecting with the audience—to get to that heightened gestalt when someone scores a goal at a soccer game. The AHHH!"

We all go into meetings at work or within our communities thinking about what we'd like to say. We usually have a pretty good idea of what we'd like to see accomplished.

That's all well and good, even if it rarely goes exactly as we plan. So what does that mean? It means that trusting your instincts to jump track and go a different direction is a talent the best communicators demonstrate at the drop of a hat.

IMPROV AND THE SCIENCE OF COMMUNICATION

Actor Alan Alda, best known as the star of the *M*A*S*H* television series, came to the State University of New York (SUNY) one summer night in 2006 to help celebrate its annual film festival and to talk about his recently published memoir, *Never Have Your Dog Stuffed*. But what he really came to talk about was his role in creating Stony Brook's Center for Communicating Science. Alda had helped create a program focusing on improvisational theater techniques and their impact on complex communication. Sixty universities across the country are now using the program, with unparalleled success.

"The idea just caught fire," Alda told his audience.

Alda wasn't new to the melding of improv with the science of communication. After the *M*A*S*H* series ended, he spent 13 years hosting a science interview program on PBS.

"Many of our guests had trouble explaining their ideas to a general audience," he noted. "So it occurred to me that the solution might be to teach scientists some basic improvisational skills."

Though improv is commonly associated with Comedy Theater, it is more fundamentally the skill of listening to an audience and making corresponding adjustments in the delivery of your message. Alda brought his idea to the SUNY President Shirley Strum Kenny; she saw the potential and arranged for Alda to meet with the school's science faculty to develop the concept.

The resulting center now attracts about 60 students a semester and is highly successful.

Alan Alda's program is most certainly an example of forward thinking on many levels, but, for me, it also reinforces how important it is for you and I to deviate from the many scripts we carry around in our heads, and the many hard and fast rules we bring into our daily lives. As I like to tell my clients, "Improvise, guys. Improvise."

Alda, and his wife, Arlene, an award winning photographer and author of 19 books, offer a series of programs honoring the power of storytelling. Her most recent book "Just Kids From The Bronx" is about Bronx memories with a nun, a police officer, an urban planner, and with Al Pacino, Carl Reiner, Colin Powell, Bobby Bonilla, Mary Higgins Clark, Regis Philbin and many other leading artists, athletes, scientists and entrepreneurs spans 6 decades of Bronx living.

Maybe your memoir is next!!!

REJECTION/FAILURE

Dr. Wayne Dyer, a man whose commentaries on life I find fascinating, says, "Failure is an editorial judgment."

You often hear people saying, "Failure is not an option."

Winston Churchill said, "success is not final, failure is not fatal; it is the courage to continue that counts."

That is certainly a paradigm shift from the "winning isn't everything, it's the only thing" mentality. It flies in the face of the "dog-eat-dog" life philosophy. And it most definitely debunks the "show me a good loser, and I'll show you a loser" school of thought.

Listen to Thomas Edison, the greatest inventor of all time: "I succeeded because I ran out of ways to fail." Babe Ruth held two seemingly contradictory records—for homeruns and strikeouts— though today he is really only remembered for the former. When someone asked the Babe what he thought about after he struck out, he shrugged his shoulders as if the answer was obvious and said, "Hitting a home run my next turn at bat."

Business and Professional development growth is much like baseball. Where else can you fail 67 percent of the time, bat .333, and go to the Hall of Fame? In other words, "just do it." If you fail or trip over some obstacle or another, just pick yourself up and do it again.

Steve Jobs said "if you are afraid of failing, you won't get very far."

NAME THIS LEADER

Here's one of my favorite guessing game questions. I call it: Name This Leader.

WHO WAS THIS LEADER?	AGE
Opened his first business—Failed	22
Ran for Legislature—Failed	23
Opened his second business—Failed	24
Elected to Legislature	25
Sweetheart died	26
Had a nervous breakdown	27
Ran for Speaker—Failed	29
Ran for Elector—Failed	31
Ran for Congress—Failed	34
Elected to Congress	37
Ran for re-election to Congress—Failed	39
Ran for Senate—Failed	46
Ran for Vice President—Failed	47
Ran for Senate—Failed	49
Elected President of the USA	51

If you guessed **Abraham Lincoln**, you're right. And one

of my favorite quotes from our 16th president is this classic: "I am a slow walker, but I never walk back."

If that's not a lesson we can apply to the theater, I don't know what is. And yes, it also works pretty darn well in the business world and on the home front.

I also like what Denzel Washington had to say about failure and rejection at a commencement speech he gave some time back:

You will fail at some point in your life; accept it. You will lose. You will embarrass yourself. You will suck at something. There is no doubt about it. That's probably not a traditional message for a graduation ceremony. But hey, I'm telling you, embrace it. Because it's inevitable. And I should know: In the acting business, you fail all the time. If you're not unemployed, you're well on your way.

Early in my career, I auditioned for a part in a Broadway musical. A perfect role for me, I thought. Well, except for the fact that I can't sing and couldn't then. So I'm in the wings, about to go on stage, and the guy in front of me is singing like Pavarotti. I'm just shrinking, getting smaller and smaller. So, I come out with my little sheet music. "Just My Imagination," by the Temptations. I hand it to the accompanist. She starts playing, and I start to sing. They're not saying anything, so I think I'm doing okay. I start getting into it. But after the first verse, the director cuts me off. He says, "Thank you. Thank you very much. You'll be hearing from me." Of course, I didn't.

But here's the thing: I didn't quit. I didn't fall back. I walked out of there to prepare for the next audition, and the next audition, and the next one. I prayed and I prayed, but I continued to fail, and I failed, and I failed.

But it didn't matter. Because you know what? You hang around a barbershop long enough, sooner or later you will get a haircut. You will catch a break. So here's the kicker. I just did a play called *Fences* and won a Tony award for it. Guess where? The Court Theater, the very same theater where I failed that first audition 30 years prior. The point is, every graduate here today has the training and the talent to succeed. But do you have the guts to fail?

I don't think Denzel Washington was just talking about the theater here, do you? I think if ever a guy delivered a message worthy of our concept of melding the worlds of theaters with those of business, leadership, and life, this was it.

Check out this next list. It shows us some very notable people who failed a time or two on their way to success and lived to tell about it:

- Ulysses S. Grant (failed in every business he ever tried until his re-enlistment in the US Army during the American Civil War)

- Michael Jordan (cut from his high school basketball team)

- Winston Churchill (failed the sixth grade)

- Thomas Edison (failed more than 2,000 times before successfully inventing the electric light)

- Ludwig Van Beethoven (music teacher told him he was hopeless as a composer)

- Walt Disney (fired by a newspaper editor because he wasn't creative enough)

- Stephen Spielberg (dropped out of high school in his sophomore year)

The points I am making here are these:

- Failure does not mean the end

- Failure can be a learning experience

- Judges of success or failure are often wrong

- Failure in one field does not mean failure in another

Or, as Fannie Flagg, actress, comedienne, author, once put it: "Don't give up before the miracle happens."

Or, as I like to say: "Always remember there's a

difference between taking a risk and taking a chance. Chance is a lottery ticket. Risk is saying, 'What's the worst thing that can happen?'" As in, what is the worst thing that can happen by auditioning for this play or by calling on this prospective client? What's the worst thing that can happen if I ask out this girl or apply for this job? If you learn to become a downside player, you'll look at the worst thing that can happen and then take the action."

In the world of business, only 10 percent of business people make more than three contacts with a prospective client and yet 80 percent of business deals are closed on the 5th to 12th contact.

FEAR

Barbara Walters once asked actor Woody Harrelson why he had chosen acting as his profession. He answered: "Because I was terrified of it." It is obvious from his response that Harrelson has an engaging, empowering, and curious relationship with discomfort and fear.

Then there is oft-repeated story about how Carol Channing got sick before every single performance of her award–winning role in *Hello Dolly*, purely out of fear, conquered it, and then blew away her audience. Now that's courage.

British-born actor Daniel Day-Lewis said about his

award- winning role as President Abraham Lincoln: "I was very shy about taking on this role. I've been tremendously privileged in being able to work in this country over the years. This idea of desecrating the memory of the most beloved president this country has ever known was just kind of a fearful thing to me."

And then there is actor Michael Douglas on his role as gay piano legend Liberace. "Even though my father was a world renowned movie star, acting wasn't on my agenda, at first. Acting didn't come naturally to me. I worked hard at it and dealt with stage fright early in my career," he said. "You go through terrible ups and downs. When I heard about the Liberace role, I first said, 'Wow, what a great challenge!' Then you hear yourself saying, 'Yeah, but can I do this?' You have a good day one day and a bad day a day later. You lose your confidence." Douglas added, "I guess the one good thing about getting older is you can say, 'Well, Michael, you've always pulled it out before. You can do it again.' But the challenge will always be there. So will the fear."

Life, love, business, leadership, the theater. The challenges are never ending. Never ending and sometimes damn scary. Fear is part of life. Overcoming fear is something we have to make part of our lives as well.

It is hard to imagine Julius Caesar fearing anything, but as he approached the river Rubicon, even he had a temporal pause. In 49 BC, crossing the river while commanding troops brought with it a death sentence from Italy for him and his men --- and, as it was, ultimately led to Civil War. Many historians still label it the greatest act of justifiable insurrection in history.

How do you handle your 'RUBICON MOMENTS?' Do you stay on the banks of the river and do nothing or do you charge forward toward your goal with a 'Take No Prisoners' attitude?

CURTAIN CALL

Preparation and practice are essentials to success, whether it's in the world of theater, the business world, or your world at home.

A little improvisation can go a long way in taking your role as an actor, businessman, spouse, or friend from the predictable to the memorable.

You have to learn to fail in order to experience victory. You have to know that failure is not the end of the world. It's often just the beginning.

Whether it's on stage or at home, sometimes it works best to present the character you're playing, and sometimes it works best to become the character.

OUT OF THE BOX OFFICE
(BERNIE'S PERSONAL CHALLENGE)

Go to a play or a movie and recognize the Drama Triangle: identify the persecutor, the victim, and the rescuer.

ACT 2

THE WORLD OF
BUSINESS

PLAYBILL

In Act 2, *The World of Business*, we will explore the world of business, or, more appropriately, the fact that we are all in business, buying or selling something every day that is either tangible or intangible: a good or service, an idea, a relationship, a strategy, a storyline. We will discover that most of us are performing some role pretty much every moment of the day. We will see how all of us have opportunities to lead, as well as those moments when we have to step back and let someone else enjoy the spotlight.

DISCOVER

- Why great business people are great performers

- How great performers make great leaders

- What makes a great performance

- Why the role of the CEO is not that different from the role of Director

LET THE SHOW BEGIN

Someone once told me that sales is the second oldest profession in the world, but I'm here to dispute that. In fact, the world's "oldest profession" clearly involves commerce. Someone has a need. Someone has a solution to that need. And our first "someone" is willing to pay the price to satisfy that need. Do the math.

The business person/entrepreneur needs to find someone who wants what he or she is offering and who is willing to pay the asking price for it. Today, sales is the highest paid profession in the world, surpassing law, medicine, and acting. So, indeed, the "oldest profession" continues to thrive.

Elmer Wheeler in the 1960's said: "Nothing happens until someone sells something." The actor must sell himself at an audition, and then must sell to an audience. If you're courting a pretty girl, you have to sell yourself as an attractive alternative to the other guy. If you're a CEO, you have to sell your team on the strategy and culture you're proposing. It's all about performing.

WHY GREAT BUSINESS PEOPLE ARE GREAT PERFORMERS

Whenever someone asks me to name the greatest business performers of the last century, I give them my all-star line-up: Andrew Carnegie of US Steel, John D. Rockefeller of Standard Oil, Henry Ford of the Ford Motor Company, Thomas Watson of IBM, Harold Geneen of ITT, Jack Welch of General Electric, and, more recently, Bill Gates of Microsoft, Steve Jobs of Apple, Jeff Bezos of Amazon, Sergey Brin and Larry Page, founders of Google and Tony Shieh, CEO of Zappos.

I believe that what sets them apart from the average business performer is a pioneering, creative, and trail-blazing spirit. They were truly pioneers, as opposed to settlers. The three major differentiators are: (1) attitudes: how they felt about themselves and their organizations in terms of their self-esteem, self-confidence, self-worth, self-image, and self-talk; (2) beliefs: in themselves and their organizations and their ability to deliver on their missions and visions; and, (3) convictions: convincing themselves and those around them that their purpose and direction were unparalleled.

WHY GREAT POLITICAL LEADERS ARE
GREAT PERFORMERS

I get the same question about my all-star lineup of the greatest political leaders in history, and my Who's Who includes: Napoleon Bonaparte; US presidents George Washington, Thomas Jefferson, John Adams, Abraham Lincoln, and Franklin D. Roosevelt; World War II leader Winston Churchill; and military officers Field Marshall Bernard Montgomery, US Generals Dwight Eisenhower, Douglas MacArthur, George Patton, and Omar Bradley; and, more recently, US Presidents Ronald Reagan and Bill Clinton (the consummate performer). All led their countries in tumultuous times.

Again, like great business performers, the three differentiators are: attitudes, beliefs, and convictions.

> "If you believe you can, or believe you can't...you're right."
>
> HENRY FORD

President Woodrow Wilson came to the White House in a meteoric rise with a short resume: President of Princeton University and two years as Governor of New Jersey. Much of US foreign policy today goes back to a speech he delivered on April 2, 1917, that focused on the belief that "the world must be made safe for democracy." The bulk of our economic policy today is based on the Federal Reserve System, which Wilson introduced. Furthermore, a

Democrat dealing with a hostile Republican audience, he maintained a constant dialogue with Congress and was able to get legislation passed because he could articulate why such legislation was necessary.

In World War I, the first modern war, Wilson took an isolationist country with an army the size of Portugal's and, within a year, had mobilized two million soldiers into the greatest fighting machine the world had seen to date and, in many ways, what Franklin Delano Roosevelt used to build on in World War II.

Franklin D. Roosevelt was a master public performer known for his frequent "Fireside Chats." The most extraordinary pictures of FDR have nothing to do with the equally extraordinary things he accomplished in his role as president. Yes, there are photos of him signing the Social Security Act into law, resolutely addressing Congress the day after the shock of the Pearl Harbor attack, and negotiating with the Allied leaders as the world descended into World War II, but the most remarkable performance shots are the ones that show him doing nothing more than standing up.

Roosevelt, who was elected president at age 50 and served until his death at age 63, never stood unassisted after the summer of 1921 when, at the age of 39, he contracted what was in his case the incongruously named infantile paralysis, or polio. Suddenly, the rising star of the Democratic Party—its vice-presidential nominee in 1920—was being dispatched to the political wilderness, a tragic figure confined to a wheelchair, who would spend the rest of his life quietly tending his family's fortune at his Hudson River estate. That's not quite how things turned out. FDR came back to win two terms as governor of New York and a stunning four terms as president of the United States, becoming one of the most consequential people ever to hold the office. He owed that resurrection, in large part, to his ability to create an illusionary theatrical performance.

When Roosevelt stood to deliver a speech, his legs were locked rigid by braces concealed by his trousers, his hands holding tight to the lectern. To his unsuspecting audience, he looked the picture of a strong and upright leader. When he waved from a balcony or railroad car or ship's deck, one hand would grab the rail or, discreetly, the arm of a military aide. He rose to throw out first pitches on opening days of the baseball season the same way. When the cameras finished snapping and the moment passed, his entourage would close in around him and help him back into his chair.

It was a series of performance scenes that, in today's era, would surely not be necessary. His wasn't the modern era, however, but one in which the image of a man who was presumed to lead had best be able-bodied. So Roosevelt, who was not above playing a role, assumed and performed in an able-bodied pose, his personal academy awards.

Winston Churchill is one of the most successful

performers in political history, serving two terms as Prime Minister of England and performances as Chancellor of the Exchequer, First Lord of the Admiralty, Home Secretary, Secretary of State for Air, Secretary of State for War, and more. He seemed to always be present at the UK's most pivotal scenes dating from the late 19th to the early 20th centuries:

> "Happiness lies in the joy of achievement and creative effort."
>
> FRANKLIN ROOSEVELT

modernizing the British Armed Forces, debating and winning the Conservative Economic cause, helping to rebuild the country after World War I, winning World War II, and rebuilding again and leading his people in the early volatile years of the Cold War. His gift was the ability to act, perform, and adapt to a variety of audiences from many different eras and find solutions to problems unique to their times.

I am a big fan of Churchill. I will never forget one of his most striking performances, when he addressed his countrymen with the infamous phrase: "NEVER, NEVER, NEVER GIVE IN". "In all things great and small, large and petty, never give in except to the conviction of honor and good sense."

Ronald Reagan, governor of California and US president, was labeled "the Great Communicator." With his clear-eyed worldview, phenomenal popular appeal, and a seamless ability to strike bargains with opponents, he was, in many ways, Roosevelt's equal. Even people who disagreed with his policies marveled at his ability to connect with them, sell them, and strike deals to implement them. An actor by profession, Reagan knew what his audiences wanted and excelled in his public debates with President Jimmy Carter and, in his re-election campaign debate, with Senator Walter Mondale. I give a lot of credit here to my close personal friend, Dr. Myles Martel, who served as his debate advisor from 1980 to 1984.

President Bill Clinton, unlike many of his predecessors, was not a transformational president, partly because the peaceful and prosperous years in which he governed did not call for grand transformation, and partly because his constant tacking to please the polls made him cautious. But he was, and remains, the most natural, innate politician/performer of the modern American era—and maybe of any era. It is a truth endlessly repeated that to chat even briefly with Clinton in a crowded room was to come away convinced that he found you the most interesting and consequential person he'd met all day. His intoxicating charm—played out both in person and before national TV

> "Myself, I am an optimist; not much sense being anything else."
> WINSTON CHURCHILL

audiences—is part of what allowed him to survive serial scandals, any of which would have sunk a lesser politician.

Finally, we have to recognize the passion and tenacity of Abraham Lincoln to lead and perform during one of the most difficult periods in

> ## "Always be clear about what you stand for."
>
> RONALD REAGAN

US history. America's most lionized president, he had to lead and perform before a wide variety of audiences—his fractious Cabinet, a contentious Congress, and a nation that had torn itself apart in a Civil War that knows no parallel in history.

I had the good fortune to be a guest of my aforementioned friend, Dr. Myles Martel, at the 150th anniversary of the Gettysburg Address on November 19, 2013, at the Gettysburg Cemetery Grounds. Dr. Martel had sponsored a statewide contest among Pennsylvania high school students who could deliver the Gettysburg Address in contemporary times. The winner of the $5,000 scholarship contest was Lauren Pyfer, a Dublin, Pennsylvania, high school sophomore who delivered an award-winning performance to an audience of some 50,000 people. Her delivery was awesome and inspiring.

WHAT MAKES A GREAT PERFORMER

Whether it's business, politics, athletics, theater, or life, the great performers set themselves above the rest by their attitudes, beliefs, convictions, discipline, goal setting, and preparation. As Benjamin Franklin said: "Failing to prepare is preparing to fail". And the great inventor Thomas Edison said, in developing the incandescent light bulb, "I succeeded because I ran out of ways to fail".

INFLUENCE

Dale Carnegie's *How to Win Friends and Influence People* had a major effect on me. My then future father-in-law Thomas F. J. Dillon, a successful real estate investor and landlord in Worcester, Massachusetts, gave the book to me while I was a senior at the University of Connecticut. Carnegie used the word "influence," but today we talk more about helping others discover what's really important. When I read this book, I thought that might be something I might want to do. After I won a football scholarship to the University of Connecticut, I was going to be an engineer. The first day

> "Nearly all men can stand adversity, but if you want to test a man's character, give him power."
>
> ABRAHAM LINCOLN

of school I had to buy a slide rule, which I couldn't afford, so I transferred over to the School of Business. The head of that school, Dean Ackerman, became my faculty advisor and encouraged me to continue in the School of Business.

This is where I first began developing an approach to business that would serve me for decades, and it was all about preparation, practice, and performing. After college, I entered the life insurance industry as a management trainee with the New York Life Insurance Company in Washington, DC. My next influential book was *How I Raised Myself from Failure to Success in Selling* by Frank Bettger. I was hooked. I remember reading a book by Elmer Wheeler entitled, *Tested Sentences That Sell,* and then *Think and Grow Rich* by Napoleon Hill.

The influences were endless. To say you can't learn anything about business and life from the pages of a book is a terrible fallacy. Yes, you have to put it into action, but the seeds are there and worth nurturing.

My father was a custodian at the Worcester Library, so I often went to work with him. He would work the 3–11 p.m. shift or the 11–7 p.m. shift, so I had the whole library to myself. He made his rounds while I read. Books became my friends. I have a library in my training center, and I encourage my trainees to borrow any book they'd like. A sign above this library expresses a long-held view of mine: "Your life will change over the next five years based on the books you read and the people you meet."

I love biographies. Learning the "why" behind the "what" is important. Why did the subject of these books become what they did? As a child, Winston Churchill was a stutterer and very self- conscious about it because the other kids made fun of him. His mother said, "Winnie, the reason you stutter is because you're so smart your brain moves faster than your lips." He listened to her and went on to become a great leader and orator.

In high school, I had a part in a play called *O! Susanna*, but my first real theater class was an evening class I enrolled in on a whim in Cambridge, Massachusetts, 25 or so years ago. We learned how to read a script. We learned the difference between monologues and dialogues. We learned to role-play. It was a blast. I didn't know anyone in the class and went there strictly as a loner. I was the senior member of the class by a long shot. I remember breaking out into groups, performing scenes, and trying to discover the message the playwright was trying to convey. Theater became a part of my life, and I've been going to plays ever since. And what I found all those years back was that the techniques I learned and the skills I began to hone on stage positively affected every job I ever worked.

When interviewing prospective hiring candidates for my clients, I always ask: "Tell me the names of the books in your personal development library?" I frequently get the body language response of M.E.G.O (my eyes glazed over!!).

This brings up an important point. You have to be willing to invest in your personal development. You have to be willing to study and read and introduce new ways of thinking into your worldview. It's all about growth and change, and these only happen in a meaningful way when you invest in yourself.

READING, LIBRARIES, ATHENAEUMS

I am a member of the Florida Speakers Association (FSA) a chapter of the National Speakers Association (NSA). We meet once a month on a Saturday from 9 a.m. to noon and always have a speaker who can help all of us grow in our speaking profession.

At a spring meeting in 2015 we had invited a group of college undergraduates to be our guest. One young lady, a sophomore at Broward College,

> ## "Successful people have Large Libraries; Unsuccessful people have Large TV's"
> ### BERNIE CRONIN

was sitting next to me at a break, so I asked her where she was from. She said Argentina. I asked her what she liked best about the United States and she knocked my socks off when she responded *"PUBLIC LIBRARIES.* You can enter at no fee, borrow hardcover and audio books at no charge, read and study, and they are in just about every town and city. We have no libraries in Argentina". I thought to myself, thank you Andrew Carnegie and the Carnegie Foundation, and everyone else in the US who has contributed to this awesome asset that many Americans take for granted. In fact, one statistic I heard was that only 3% of Americans have a Library Card. Much of this book you are reading was written at the Public Library in Boynton Beach, Florida.

In the summer we vacation on Cape Ann, 35 miles north of Boston where there are public libraries in every town on Cape Ann including Beverly, Beverly Farms, Manchester By The Sea (1887), Gloucester, Rockport, Essex (1893), Ipswich and the community owned Magnolia Library Center of which I am proud to have served as President. With a great group of Board members we paid off our debt with functions, events, festivals and musicals and it continues to thrive today.

My favorite town in Florida, where for many years I had an office, is Palm Beach, 20 miles north of our home in Boynton Beach, Florida. Home to many great restaurants, the 5 Star Breakers Hotel, The Henry Morrison Flagler Museum, great beaches and more. Prominent residents include singers Jimmy Buffet and Rod Stewart, The Billionaire Koch Brothers, Author James Patterson, Donald Trump and many more but…..NO PUBLIC LIBRARY! I wonder why???

An Athenaeum is defined as 1. An institution for the promotion of literary 2. A library or reading room. In ancient Athens it was a place in which professors taught and actors or poets rehearsed.

The only Athenaeum I know is located at 10½ Beacon Street in downtown Boston. Founded in 1807 by a group of high-brow Bostonians – the nephew of President John Adams was its first librarian – the Athenaeum was built on the idea that the city's deepest thinkers needed a place to read, discuss ideas and take in cultural events. Almost from the start it prospered.

Its 19th Century splendor of high ceilings, marble busts and spiral staircases houses much of George Washington's personal library, genuine Lewis & Clark artifacts, and still schedules afternoon tea.

With a membership made up largely of wealthy locals, the library became a gathering place for the area's elite. Over the past two centuries its collection has swelled to include more than 500,000 circulating books and 150,000 rare titles.

This venerable institution has adjusted to the times of the Baby Boomers, Gen X, Gen Y and Millennials, and now hosts craft beer nights, oyster tastings and even an April Fool's Day Party. (Source Boston Globe)

THE RULE OF 7 +/– 2

I first realized the role of theater in business when I was working as an executive for Information Mapping Inc. (IMI), a company located in Waltham, Massachusetts, founded by Dr. Robert Horn, a professor who taught at Harvard University.

Dr. Horn developed a methodology for writing from the reader's point of view (or the audience), not the writer's point of view (or a matter of "here's all I know"). It was my first hands-on experience with a methodology (a set of principles), and it got me to thinking about what a business development methodology would look like.

One of Horn's methodology rules is the Rule of 7 +/– 2, which I continue to apply in my coaching and consulting work and follow today in my writing as well. The rule is based on the way in which the brain processes information and relates to information in groups of seven, plus or minus two. For example, we remember phone numbers in chunks of seven digits. Social security numbers are groups of seven. Bank routing numbers are   made up of 9 digits (or 7+2), whereas zip codes are five digits (or 7-2). We learn the alphabet in chunks of seven, as in: a, b, c, d, e, f, g; and there are, of course, 7 days in a week, 7 Continents, 7 Seas, 7 Deadly Sins, 7 Notes in music, 7 Colors in a rainbow and Steven Covey's *7 Habits of Highly Effective People.*

And please note, I've written this book in nine chapters (7+2). Aristotle offered his own view of this when he said, "All human actions have one or more of these seven causes: chance, nature, compulsion, habit, reason, passion, and desire." There's that emotional driver again, the infamous

Drama Triangle.

Whether you believe in the Rule of 7 +/- 2 is not as important as having your own system, your own plan, your own layout, and your methodology; something that works for you, and something you believe in irrevocably.

LIVE AND LEARN

While at IMI, I decided to continue my education and enrolled in the Harvard University Extension School, where I took courses in Business and Organization Communications and Microcomputers and Information Technologies (way over my head).

One evening after class, I came across the Cambridge Center for Adult Education and decided to enroll in a course titled Acting for Beginners, taught by longtime acting coach, playwright, and producer Stan Edelson.

In my business career to this point, I had subconsciously related business to acting and theater and just didn't realize it. How? In my dress (costume), my talk-track or script (performance), and my cast of characters. On large client business interviews, I always made it a point to role-play (rehearse) the lines and actions of the team's characters, who were the lead role and supporting roles, how and when the leader "passed the baton" to another cast member, and how that cast member would re-pass the baton back to the leading man or lady.

In the end, this all goes back to preparation and practice for an award-winning performance, whether it's a corporate decision, a business development interview, opening night, or the next step in your life.

BERNIE'S BROADWAY DEBUT?

Anyone who has worked with me over the years has heard me say many times: *"Showtime!!"* I believe it. I know my forays into the world of theater made me a better businessman and coach, and a more open and honest spouse and friend.

Here are the steps that I followed on this circuitous route:

Step 1: In 2001, a client who had recently moved from Boston to New York called me and said, "You have to come to New York and meet my new Acting Coach, Anthony Bova." So I did. And I attended one of his all-day Acting Training Sessions in the Eric Morris System, for which he is the exclusive New York-based instructor and East Coast authority. When I returned to Boston, I had a greater understanding of the roles of theater and drama in the sales and business environment. It was a great beginning.

Anthony had some interesting methodology. For example, he had us lie on the floor and limber up and work on being our own instruments. We did a lot of primal moaning to get rid of our inhibitions and to get relaxed. One time he said to me, "Bernie, how do you feel?"

I said, "I feel a little nervous".

He kept asking me this. "How do you feel?"

I finally said, "I feel stupid. I feel like I should be playing golf with a bunch of old farts in Florida. How do I feel? I don't even know the people in here. I feel stupid that I'm even here".

"Keep going!"

The more I got in touch with "How do I feel?" the more I was able let go of my tension. It was a great exercise for relaxing my instrument and preparing for my role. I was ready to become somebody that I wasn't. It really helped me overcome the inhibition of being in front of someone doing something that was totally foreign to anything I'd ever done before. Snarling at 30 or 40 people felt good, like letting go of my head trash. It was like, "Come on, Bernie. This is theater. This is improv. This is preparation. This is connecting and communicating".

It made me want to get better at my craft in business and to do that I needed to learn the craft of acting. Why? Because I realized I was really a full-time actor in my job.

Whenever I do a Keynote Speech or a presentation to a company to retain my coaching services, I blend theater with business. That's show biz. Often times when I go on a prospective client interview, I'll say to myself, "It's showtime, Bernie!"

Step 2: I invited Anthony to come to Boston and attend and participate in my weekly program. He was a willing participant and added an energy that was infectious. I realized what a terrific connection we'd made.

Step 3: Anthony and I created a working collaboration. This represented the early stage of a process that saw Anthony modifying the Morris System and creating his own Bova Communication System. During this time, Anthony delivered communication techniques based on the Eric Morris System to my clients, and we successfully offered a number of one-day sessions at my Boston Theater. Very cool stuff.

Anthony and I said, "Let's put something together. Let's put an acting class together." So we put together classes in Boston for my clients. We taught several one-day acting classes, and that's when I first thought about melding acting and business and professional development.

Step 4: This was my decision in 2004 to enroll in a weekend session of Eric Morris's once-a-year weekend boot camp for actors in New York City. I had a number of "negative" thoughts about doing this, like: (1) I'm not a professional actor, so what am I doing here? (2) How will I relate to these hippie, artsy, young, liberal thinking actors? (3) What's an "old duffer" like me doing in a weekend acting class on the 11th floor in a studio on 49th Street and Broadway when I should be on the golf course with my Florida buddies?

Step 5: In 2007, I created an invitation-only program for clients of mine with Ronald Reagan Debate Advisor and advisor to the White House Office of Communications Dr. Myles Martell and Anthony Bova. We brought in a number of people for a long weekend, and they stayed at the Colony Hotel in Palm Beach. We used the G-Star of the Arts, a charter school in West Palm Beach, Florida, for our theater all day Saturday and part of Sunday. We finished up with golf at my club.

During the course of the weekend, Myles did the leadership legacies of Ronald Reagan, I did Theatre and Business Systems, and Anthony did the Acting System developed by Eric Morris.

For example, we had the clients perform scenes from any number of different screenplays and read Winston Churchill's speech "Never Give In," reading it aloud with emotion.

The entire collaboration with Myles and Anthony was an eye-opening experience that confirmed the similarities between the worlds of theater, business, corporate management, leadership, and, not to forget, life in general.

Step 6: This step occurred in April 2008 when I was introduced to acting coach and Blue Man Group performer Frank Licari and his Atlantic Arts Center in Jupiter, Florida.

Frank was a member of the original Blue Man Group in Boston and a master trainer of improv. Frank and I collaborated on a number of projects incorporating acting, leadership, and life and discovered along the way that people play many roles in their lives, and the better prepared we are for them, the better versed we become in fulfilling those roles. We still offer these programs today in South Florida and at corporate sites anywhere in the world.

Step 7: In 2012, I joined the Emerging Playwrights Group at the Burt Reynolds Institute for Film and Theater. We met for three consecutive months on Thursdays and were taught by one of Burt's protégées. It was all about the role of the playwright and how to dissect a play. We would perform different scenes and study them to discover the message the playwright was trying to convey and how he developed characters. Burt Reynolds conducted a class himself one night and was terrific. He walked on the stage and talked for three straight hours about movies and theater and how he'd prepared for *Deliverance* and *The Longest Yard*. It expanded my knowledge of theater and of acting in a way only a fellow actor could do.

PEPSICO'S DALLAS DEBUT

Candy Buckley, a Broadway stage actor is onstage portraying a martini-swilling 57 year old mother. *"I want to be healthy but I also want a martini,"* laments Buckley's character.

"I'm torn".

Is this the Neil Simon Theatre? Off Broadway? No, it's the Embassy Suites in Rogers, Ark. Wal-Mart Country.

Shakespeare it's not, but the staging is part of an effort by Pepsi to show its retailers and its own sales force that it's on a health crusade. Faced with flat sales from carbonated beverages Pepsi has been trying to balance revenues from what it calls "fun for you" food like soda and snacks with "good for you" foods like Quaker Soy Crisps. But changing the DNA of a $35 billion soda and salty snacks giant was no easy feat, even internally. "PowerPoint presentations wouldn't do" said Antonio Lucio, the Pepsico Executive spearheading the effort. The company had to do something, well....DRAMATIC! So Lucio brought in trend guru, Faith Popcorn for help. When she floated the idea of turning Pepsi's market research into theater, he agreed.

Getting a reluctant, two-time Drama Desk Award nominee, Alex Dinelaris, to join the team, Pepsi poured $1.5 million into the project.

Armed with stacks of demographic tables and reports on consumer buying trends, Dinelaris came up with a series of one-act shows, each of which depicts an American character with unhealthy eating habits or a health-related crisis; a working mom worried about her overweight son's diet; an ex-jock who injures himself at the gym on his 45th birthday.

The plays debuted in Dallas in front of an audience of Pepsico Executives–including CEO Indra Nooyi. Popcorn and Dinelaris knew they had a hit when Nooyi herself told Dinelaris that she saw a few executives actually tear up. Nooyi is an Indian-born, naturalized American business executive and current Chairperson and CEO of PepsiCo, the second largest food and beverage business in the world.

Soon after Lucio booked a multicity tour of the PepsiCo Show!!

Today a number of corporations are incorporating drama and musicals into conveying their messages to employees and customers.

THE SEVEN PARTS OF SELF

I teach people about the seven parts of the self.

Number one: Self-esteem is how I feel about myself. If I don't love myself, then I can't love others. If I don't love myself, then others won't love me. Sometimes, I play golf with people who beat themselves up. After a bad shot, they say to themselves, "You stupid bozo". I ask them, "Why do you say that to yourself? You're a nice person, but just a lousy golfer. Don't do this to yourself". Then I ask them "would you let anyone else talk to you the way you talk to yourself?"

Healthy self-esteem means I love myself and feel good

about what I do. If I hold the door open for an elderly lady with a walker, I don't need to get rewarded, because this was something I wanted to do. I feel good about myself for sitting down with people and encouraging them to get out of their comfort zone, without any economic benefit to me or needing credit for this on my Playbill.

Number two: Self-image is how I see myself. I see myself as a winner not a loser. I see myself as reaching the top of the mountain and obtaining my goal. I play to win, not to lose.

Number three: Self-concept is how I conceive of myself as a person. This isn't predicated on how others see me, but rather comes from within.

Number four: Self-worth is how I value myself. Again, this is not dependent on how others value me, but comes from within.

Number five: Self-doubt centers on the doubts I have about myself. What negatives do I have? What do I doubt that I can do? What do I not attempt because I doubt that I can be successful at it?

Number six: Self-confidence focuses on my ability to accomplish the goal or goals I set for myself. There's a difference between confidence and cockiness. A cocky person sends his mother and father a congratulatory note on his birthday. Confident people don't have to tell anyone that they are confident. They don't brag or boast; they simply exude confidence.

Number seven: Self-talk is how I talk to myself, at the rate of 800 words a minute. According to Chad Helmstetter in his book *What You Say When You Talk to Yourself*, 77 percent of this talk is negative: "I could never do that. I couldn't reach that person. I could never do business with them …".

> "My definition of success is accepting fear, feeling it, and dealing with it."
>
> BERNIE CRONIN

Replace this with positive self-talk and the sky is the limit: "I can do it. I'm the little engine that could." Positive self-talk is a great tool and you need to develop affirmations in the present tense: "I am successful. I am getting there. I am getting better. I expand in abundant success and love every day and encourage those around me to do the same. Oh, yeah, and one last thing: Don't use the term "try". It's a useless word. I also like to list the seven most important things I have to do today. If you don't have a plan, you will default to someone else's plan. As Benjamin Franklin said, "Failing to prepare is preparing to fail".

After you've made a detailed plan, prepare to improvise. Don't be so rigid that you can't adapt to the audience. Maybe there's someone at your meeting who you didn't think would be there, and now you have to improvise. Or there are interruptions, or your timeframe might be shortened so you have to make a shortened presentation. Improv is great training for business, because things change so frequently and you have to learn to move on your toes.

At meetings, I never have two people sitting on one side of the table across from two more on the other side. Then, it becomes us against them. I sit next to the person whose meeting and have my partner do the same. That is again all about setting your stage.

> "Culture is the sum of an organization's values and what they are truly about. Culture trumps strategy every time."
>
> BERNIE CRONIN

The other thing we need to focus on with both theater and business and personal development is coaching. Most great actors have coaches. Most great athletes have a coach. People have personal trainers and personal development coaches. Business owners have life coaches now.

Whenever I walk into the lobby of an organization for the first time, or go to their website, I always look for their mission statement. Many companies have statements like,

"We're bigger, we're better, we're faster. Our mission is to be the best possible supplier of dental equipment."

That's a statement of why they exist—not a mission statement. The best example I've ever seen of a mission is Google's twelve words: "To organize the world's information and make it universally accessible and useful." These people know what they are doing.

CURTAIN CALL

- A few moments of positive self-talk will take you further than all the negativity in the world.

- If you want to be a first-class leader, then you have to learn to be a first-class performer.

- Fear, uncertainty, and doubt are all part of the gig; walking on stage is the first step in coming to terms with them and using them to your benefit.

- Showtime is a state of mind. It's not a person, place, or thing.

- It's the performer in you trying to get out.

OUT OF THE BOX OFFICE
(BERNIE'S PERSONAL CHALLENGE)

Write down the names of the seven people you most admire, living or dead. They could be parents, teachers, mentors, athletes, business leaders, religious leaders, political leaders, theatrical celebrities, etc.

Put a dominant characteristic next to each name. Now write in next to the characteristic whether it is an (A) ATTITUDE or (B) SKILLS.

In most cases, ATTITUDE will be checked more than SKILLS.

"The role of the actor is to take action consistent with that of the character he/she has become. To perform and behave in a way the audience totally identifies with and accepts as the messenger of the character's beliefs."

BERNIE CRONIN

ACT 3

ROLES OF THE ACTOR

PLAYBILL

In Act 3, Roles of the Actor, we will explore how actors prepare for the theater, how they integrate with other actors, how they interact with the director and the producer, and how they "become" their characters. We will delve into the role of the "actor" as it relates to the C-Level Suite, the office, and the factory floor. We will see just how each and every one of us takes on a different role as we move from the workplace out into the community, and again when we step into our homes and become parents or spouses, sons and daughters, brothers and sisters.

DISCOVER

- Why there are no insignificant actors in any play or any setting

- How the best leaders are really actors in disguise

- How we all take on roles at home and in the community

- Where and how we prepare for these roles

LET THE SHOW BEGIN

Have you ever seen a movie about the world of business where its leading man or woman is characterized as professional, courteous, loving, and caring? As people you would look up to as a result of their chosen profession? As people who contribute greatly to their communities? The answer is a resounding NO! This is unfortunate, but there is also a lot to be learned from this fact.

Just think about the behavioral traits attributed to the main characters in some of the most famous business development movies of all time:

- *Death of a Salesman*—The sad story of a salesman, Willy Loman, at the end of his career, is based on the Pulitzer Prize-winning play written by Arthur Miller. Actor Lee J. Cobb played in the first Broadway production, followed by numerous other actors on stage and screen. I saw the play in both New York and Boston with Brian Dennehy as the lead and had tears in my eyes. Dennehy captured the pivotal scene perfectly when Willy implores his son with some particularly poor advice. "Biff," he says. "It's not important to be just liked, but to be really liked." I call this psychological trait a "HIGH NEED FOR APPROVAL," and it is the downfall of many in the world of business. *Glengarry Glen Ross* — Epic movie about a group of regional sales reps fighting to save their jobs while their over-the-top boss puts the screws to them. It stars Alec Baldwin, Jack Lemmon, and Al Pacino. Baldwin, as the sales manager, is constantly bullying his sales team and berating them with vulgarities and putdowns, while his sales team counters with charges of lousy sales leads. It's a classic case of how not to perform in sales meetings and how to "de-incentivize" your team. In this movie, Baldwin plays the persecutor and the sales team play the victims (the drama triangle). Interestingly, there is no Rescuer.

- *Jerry Maguire* — Movie about a professional

player agent fighting to save his career after going against the grain of his fellow agents. The movie stars Tom Cruise as Jerry Maguire and Cuba Gooding as professional football player Rod Tidwell. Jerry makes famous the line, "Show me the money," while discovering that the true decision maker in many transactions is not who you think it might be. Jerry figures out that in Rod's case, it's really his wife, thus coining the phrase: "Closed her!"

- *Tin Men* — A Danny DeVito film in which he and Richard Dreyfus are competitors selling aluminum siding. The heart of the movie concerns all the dirty tricks they play on each other. These guys are selling aluminum home siding and hard-selling the prospects with features and benefits and never asking any emotional questions. In this movie, they portray the "show up and throw up" approach. They portray what we think of as the typical fast-talking, back slapper... Not typical at all.

- *Boiler Room* — This is a movie about fast-talking rip-off artists conning prospects into buying junk bonds on the phone. It is a perfect example of shoving a product down a prospect's throat for a single purpose: making a quick buck.

- *The Goods: Live Hard, Sell Hard*—Hilarious movie starring Jeremy Piven as a hired gun brought in to save a car dealership from going under. Many tongue-in- cheek situations and behind-the-scenes views.

These are all good movies. *Boiler Room* and *Glengarry Glen Ross* are among the best and worst characterizations of client development. Some others worth watching, if only for fun, are *The Prime Gig, Traveling Man, Used Cars, The Closer, The Hot Spot, Diamond Men, Tommy Boy, New Age,* and *Tucker*. A couple of business movies that I like are *Billionaire Boys Club, Barbarians at the Gate,* and *Pirates of Silicon Valley*.

Amazingly, there are actually companies out there that use many of the movies listed above as training tools for their sales and marketing forces, rather than as cautionary messages about what not to do! Believe it or not, there are many people out there who think that professional, consultative business people act just like Alec Baldwin in *Glengarry Glen Ross* or Danny DeVito in *Tin Men*—and it's just not true. You might want to add *Wall Street* with Michael Douglas and *The Wolf of Wall Street* with Leonardo DiCaprio to this list of characterizations.

There is one other film I just have to mention. It is a story Barbara Walters did on a real-life paralyzed door-to-door salesman in Oregon, called *A Moving Journey*. It will bring tears to your eyes and make you realize your problems are nothing compared to this man's problems, which he overcomes to realize his success.

THE ROLE OF THE "ACTOR" IN BUSINESS

> "You can't buy a reputation, but you can sell one."
>
> BERNIE CRONIN

I wasn't aware of the role of acting as it relates to the business world and to leadership back in the mid-1980s when I was the manager for the Boca Raton, Florida, office of FCA Asset Management, a subsidiary of what was, at that time, the largest savings and loan company in the country, American Savings & Loan. Our job was to solicit Jumbo Certificates of Deposit in the amount of $100,000 or more from institutional investors, such as other banks, savings and loans companies, credit unions, insurance companies, and corporations and foundations.

Since we weren't licensed in Florida to accept deposits, all of our solicitations were done by phone, all over the country, and all monies had to be deposited via wire transfer to our Stockton, California, home office. We were not allowed by corporate policy to solicit individual depositors.

Every day when I was driving to my office in Boca via Highland Beach, I would pass miles and miles of mansions and million-dollar condos. Every day I thought the same thing: These people were prospects we should be cultivating. Most certainly they owned one or more Jumbo CDs anyway, and would almost certainly love to get a higher rate from their bank. That's just human nature.

After thinking about this for a while, I developed a business plan and presented it to the president of our subsidiary, asking permission to solicit individual accounts in South Florida. In my presentation (aka, my performance), I estimated that there was likely more individual money from Key Biscayne to Vero Beach, east of the Intercoastal Waterway, than along any other comparable stretch of real estate in the country.

The president bought my plan, but swore me to secrecy. This was to be an exception to the general rules of the company and, thus, just between the two of us.

After that, I requested and received a budget to hire five part-time teleprospectors to call wealthy homeowners in the early evenings during the week, and from 9 a.m. to 1 p.m. on Saturdays. Once the budget was in place, I had to figure out where to find these part-time phone solicitors and train them in "call scripts" and in using banking terminology. The logical place seemed to be the business school of the local college, Florida Atlantic University (FAU), about two miles from my office.

I made an appointment with the dean of the department,

but when I arrived, the receptionist said, "I'm sorry Mr. Cronin, but we'll have to reschedule. The dean was called into an emergency meeting. We left a message at your office, but you must not have gotten it."

I walked out and started back to my car. Yes, I was disappointed. But I also noticed that I still had time on my Visitor's Parking pass. Why waste it? I looked around and saw a building marked SCHOOL of DRAMA and MUSIC. Like all business people, I hate rejection and didn't want to go home empty-handed a la Willy Loman.

"What the hell?" I said looking at the building. "Why not give it a try?"

So I went inside and explained my mission to the Assistant Dean of the School of Drama and Music. Guess what he said? "You've come to the right place, Mr. Cronin. My people would love to perform in that role. When would you like to start *auditioning*?"

Wow, did this gentleman understand what I was after. His students knew nothing about banking, CDs, maturities, interest rates, rollovers, or FDI insurance, and this turned out to be a blessing. What they did understand was the idea of connecting with people, and that's what I wanted.

I hired five students from the department, three women and two men. Their job was to prospect high net-worth individuals living along the prescribed beach corridor.

Part of their training was to develop, rehearse, and role-play phone scripts. Once our rehearsals were over, we launched our debut in what I called my Boca Raton Phone Center Theater. They were excellent at playing their roles and interacting with potential new customers, exercising skills that melded acting and performing with selling and marketing. After nine months, we had all the business we could process and had to terminate the program. Talk about a success. Those were some of the best hires I ever made. I trained them and then let them do their jobs—a good leadership tip.

In those days, there were about 12,000 banks in the United States and only about 200 of them had assets over a billion dollars. After launching the Boca Raton Phone Center Theater, my office was almost as big as some of those 200 banks.

This is an example of business and the theater being tied together in the most literal way. Acting is about connecting. So is business. If you can't connect with your end user—your audience if you're in a play, and your customer if you're in business—then you're bound to fall short in either case.

In the theater, there are hundreds of people involved in getting a play off the ground; not all of them can act and not all of them can monitor the lighting, but they are all important once the curtain goes up. In business, not everyone understands product development and not everyone understands a balance sheet, but they are all important to the bottom line. My team didn't know a thing about CDs. I didn't need them to. I just needed them to be a connection to the people we were soliciting. And it worked. Shortly thereafter, I was recruited away by the largest independent commercial bank in Florida, formed my own company—I called it Bankers Marketing Corporation, using my initials BMC as a promotional tool—and successfully helped banking institutions and other investment firms grow their deposit bases and build pro-active client development cultures.

Since then, I have been doing coaching, consulting and Keynote Speaking in more than 200 different industries. Each and every time one of my clients sets out to develop some method of phone prospecting or to develop a call center of some type, I always advise them, "Go to the local college and recruit your team from their drama and music departments". In Boston, it's the Berklee School of Music. In Connecticut, it's the Yale Drama School. In Rhode Island, it's the Rhode Island School of Design. In South Florida, it's the School of Drama at Nova Southeastern University. You get the idea.

This leads me to a story about Warren Bennis, former president of the University of Cincinnati, gifted writer, and extraordinary storyteller. Bennis wrote about leadership in a most inventive way and presented his ideas in front of hundreds of rapt audiences. He loved to juxtapose "performance and reinvention" in his writing and illustrate it in his storytelling.

His is a great story well described in *The Essential Bennis*.

He tells of a klutzy 8th grader who panicked when given an assignment to talk in class about his favorite hobby, mainly because he didn't have one. Then he remembered the only physical activity that he regularly engaged in was—drum roll, please—shining shoes. When the day came for his presentation, he stood up and spoke at length about, yes, shoe polish. He explained in detail the subtle differences between the colors of maroon and oxblood while discussing the advantages of solid versus liquid wax.

In a flash, Warren Bennis, storyteller, raconteur, and presenter, was born. No longer the lonely, morose kid who felt like the only Jew in Westwood, New Jersey, he was suddenly a confident storyteller who'd engaged his classmates and won the approval of Miss Shirer, the teacher he had long adored.

"It was a remarkable performance," Bennis wrote many years later, "if only because it was, from start to finish, an act of pure imagination."

In another piece called *Leadership as a Performing Art*, Bennis wrote, "The ability to act—as in theater—influences every aspect of leadership in every arena, from the playground to the boardroom."

Whether it's leadership or life, we prosper with the recognition of the various roles we create for ourselves. We're not talking about faking the person we really are; we're saying that every one of us has many sides, and we should maximize the depth of who we are. Know your many sides and embrace them.

PROFESSIONALS, ATHLETES, AND THE ART OF ACTING

The Essential Bennis can best be seen in professionals such as lawyers, doctors, psychiatrists, psychologists, clergymen, and athletes; they all perform various roles throughout their day, and those who perform those roles most effectively usually come out on top.

> ## "Miracles don't happen overnight; sometimes they take an entire year."
>
> BERNIE CRONIN

Think of the award-winning performances that attorneys Johnnie Cochran and F. Lee Bailey put on during the O. J. Simpson trial, getting one of the quickest verdicts in one of the longest running trials of all time. Right or wrong, they performed, and their audience responded.

Hall of Fame tennis legend Chris Evert once explained it this way: "When you're famous at a young age, you get labeled a certain way before you really develop as a person. The press calls you 'Little Miss Ice Maiden' or 'Cinderella on Sneakers.' That kind of thing. I was labeled as sort of being a 'goody-goody' and not having much emotion. It puts you in a bubble. And sometimes you have a tendency to act that out because you know that's what is expected of you by your audience. The trademark of my game was the mental part and my concentration and preparation. I pretty much had tunnel vision when I was out there. I didn't let anything affect me. I was unemotional on the court because that worked for me. Off the court, it was a lot different."

> "The game of golf is like the game of life; some good shots turn into bad shots, some bad shots turn into good shots, and you play it where it lies."
>
> BOBBY JONES

I once played golf in a foursome with Hall of Famer Joe Namath. During the round, I asked him how he'd prepared for those two-minute drills he was so famous for late in games.

"Just before practice ended every day," he told me, "Don Maynard [his favorite receiver] and I would go to the two-yard line and throw 50 passes. We had to complete 50 in a row before we could go to the locker room. In game situations, we were so conditioned and prepared we just executed what we perfectly prepared for in our role."

Serena Williams, holder of 11 Major Singles Titles and 11 Major Doubles titles, including Wimbledon and the US Open, is known for exhibiting astounding composure in the toughest, competitive tennis situations. However, Williams dismisses such toughness and says, "There are plenty of things in life that make me nervous and frightful, like acting in *ER* or *Law and Order*. Now that's nerve-wracking."

Golfing legend Bobby Jones said, "Golf is not just a game, but a subject worthy of study." And study and perform he did.

Phil Jackson won more championships than any coach in the history of professional sports. He is arguably the greatest coach in the history of the NBA. His reputation was established as head coach of the Chicago Bulls from 1989 to 1998; during his tenure, Chicago won six NBA titles. His next team, the Los Angeles Lakers, won five NBA titles from 2000 to 2010.

Jackson was tagged the "Zen Master" by sportswriters. Though half in jest, the nickname speaks to an important truth: This is a coach who inspired, not goaded. He led by awakening and challenging his players to perform at a level far beyond mediocrity. Los Angeles Lakers star Rick Fox describes Phil Jackson's approach to acting as "a play in three acts." Act 1 was the first 20 or 30 games of each 82-game season, when Jackson would sit back and let the characters reveal themselves. Act 2 would take place during the 20 or 30 games during the middle of the season, before and after the All-Star game. That's when he would nurture the team, when guys were starting to get bored. Act 3 would take place during the last 20 or 30 games leading up to the playoffs and, according to Fox, Jackson's whole demeanor would change— the way he looked, talked, and moved—as if he was saying, "This is my time." "In the run up to the playoffs, Phil gave us new confidence and an identity we didn't have before and take the pressure off of us and put it on himself," says Fox. I share these examples with you because they collectively illustrate the common ground between commitment, passion, perseverance, and discipline— both in one's professional life and one's personal life. You don't have to be an athlete to understand this. You don't have to be an artist. You just have to be someone dedicated to achieving something special, creating the best possible relationships you can have, and taking action in a world dominated by inaction and reaction.

Actors take up this task every time they go on stage. You can't just sit there. You have to perform. You have to rise above your fears and give your audience something to cheer about or relate to. The truth is, everyone is acting most of the time.

COSTUMES

As I mentioned earlier, when we get up in the morning or plan the night before, we select our costume to best connect with our audience that day. Is it a white shirt, business dress for a banker meeting or Birkenstocks and jeans for a software developer? I have sometimes changed costumes 2 and 3 times during a day depending upon my audience. By the way,

I love Black Tie events and can't wait to attire myself in my tuxedo, vest, black shoes, etc. In my acting classes with Frank Licari I wear my black pants, black shirt, black flat top hat and sunglasses…..totally uncharacteristic to those who know me well.

Renowned London-based costumier, Angels, celebrating its 175th year of its business in costumes in 2015, ranks some of the following in their Top 50 in movies as follows:

- CLEOPATRA (1963) played by Elizabeth Taylor

- FIRST BLOOD (1982) Rambo played by Sylvester Stallone

- THE GOOD, THE BAD AND THE UGLY (1966) played by Clint Eastwood

- WILLY WONKA and THE CHOCOLATE FACTORY (1971) played by Gene Wilder

- DRACULA (1931) played by Bela Lugosi

- GHOSTBUSTERS (1984) played by Bill Murray

- BREAKFAST AT TIFFANYS (1961) played by Audrey Hepburn

- EASY RIDER (1969) played by Peter Fonda

- THE 7 YEAR ITCH (1955) played by Marilyn

Monroe

- TOPGUN (1986) played by Tom Cruise

- TOOTSIE (1982) played by Dustin Hoffman

- INDIANA JONES AND THE RAIDERS OF THE LOST ARK (1981) played by Harrison Ford

- DR. SEUSS' HOW THE GRINCH STOLE CHRISTMAS (2000) played by Jim Carrey

- THE GRAND BUDAPEST HOTEL (2014) played by Ralph Fiennes

- REBEL WITHOUT A CAUSE (1955) played by James Dean

THE ACTOR'S CREDO

I don't know if Ralph Waldo Emerson was talking about actors and actresses when he wrote this quote, but I love it: "Do the thing you fear and the death of fear is certain."

Think about it. Take the risk, get it over with, and then step aside.

Surround yourself with people who truly want you to succeed. A lot of people will want to stay in their comfort zone and keep you in your comfort zone. Find those who are going to

encourage you to break out and take a risk. And always know the difference between taking a risk and taking a chance. Chance is betting on a horse. Taking a risk is acting out a long-range strategy.

How many of you have written down your goals? Do it. Now. Most people spend more time planning their vacation than they do their life.

I once met a very successful investor in Florida who owned more railroad cars than anyone in the country. He had a ton of money. After he bought a bank in Florida, he hired me to work with him. "You're a very successful financial guy." I said to him. "What's the key to your success?"

"I am a downside player, Bernie. I always look at the worst thing that can possibly happen by taking a risk and making a decision. I know the worst case going in, and I know I can survive it. When I bought this bank, the worst outcome was that I could lose a million dollars."

He quickly found out that he didn't like banking or banking regulators, so he sold the bank and lost the million dollars he was willing to risk. When the worst happened, he didn't blame the outcome on chance or bad luck. He didn't see himself as a victim. He learned his lesson and went on to the next deal.

VISUALIZE, PLAN, EXAMINE

Whether you're an actor, a CEO, or a housewife, here are Bernie's steps for turning your vision into reality.

Sometimes I write myself a note that reads "I'm not worthy. I don't deserve success." And then I go to the shedder in my office and run the note through it. It's gone.

> ## "Failure is okay. Not attempting something is not okay."
> ### BERNIE CRONIN

Out of my head, out of my heart. It's like a vacuum cleaning for your brain. Get the head trash out of there. I have a small, tabletop bright orange trash can in my training center with a swivel top you can deposit small pieces of paper in. I hand blank pieces of paper to my clients and have them write down negative thoughts they find themselves subconsciously saying to themselves, the "negative self-talk", and then they deposit the negative thought into the shredder to symbolically rid themselves of the negative thoughts.

> ## "Have the courage to fail."
> ### BERNIE CRONIN

I also have what I call "Q-tips" for people who have to make prospecting cold calls. "Q-tip" stands for "Quit taking it personally." It's a little reminder that blame and fault get you nowhere.

Here's the key. Whether you're an actor, a business person, or a kid asking a girl to homecoming, remember this: No one can reject me without my permission. How you feel about me is none of my business. How I feel about me is my business.

MOTIVATION (MOTIVE FOR ACTION)

On the first day of my previously described banking client development position at FCA Asset, I was stymied. I just shuffled my cards, went to the bathroom, and drank hot coffee. You can't make cold calls without hot coffee! I went home that night and said to my wife, Helen, "I just couldn't do it. I couldn't pick up the phone. I couldn't make myself call a bunch of strangers. I think I'm going to call in tomorrow and resign."

My daughter Maura, a sophomore in high school, heard this conversation and decided to give me her perspective. She walked in and said to me, "I heard you and Mom talking about your reluctance to pick up the phone and cold call your clients. I hope you can get over it. I didn't tell you this, but I want to go to the University of Vermont. I'm going to need your help paying for this. I'm going to go back to school tomorrow and get the best grades I can. I want you to agree to go back to your office tomorrow and make those calls. Deal?"

So what do you suppose I did the next day? I picked up that phone and started dialing. I wasn't going to look my daughter in the eye on graduation day from high school and say, "Maura, you can't go to the University of Vermont because your father is a wimp."

I picked up the phone and said, "Hi, this is Bernie Cronin from American Savings. I've got a 4 percent rate on a million dollars or more for six months. Are you in the market?"

That was it. I started with a million-dollar investment on each call and ended up with a portfolio of more than a billion dollars— because I got over what I have since labeled "call reluctance." I replaced reluctance with MOTIVATION (motive for action)!!

CURTAIN CALL

- Visualize where you want to go, create a plan for getting there, and examine your plan regularly.

- Recognize the roles you have to play and don't be afraid to play them.

- No one can do it alone. The actor needs the stagehand just as much as the CEO needs the janitor.

- Respect yourself even when you fail.

OUT OF THE BOX OFFICE
(BERNIE'S PERSONAL CHALLENGE)

Locate the School of Drama and Theater in local colleges and universities in your area and hire student interns in roles that require a great deal of human interactions: call centers, customer service, reception, phone inquiries, etc., and let me know how it works out.

> *"The role of the business person is to get the prospect or client to take action consistent with action they believe they should take, for their benefit, and for which they will pay the business person their price."*

BERNIE CRONIN

ACT 4

ROLES OF BUSINESS PERFORMERS

PLAYBILL

In Act 4, Roles of Business Performers, we will explore the roles that men and women play in their business and professional worlds, how their scripts are written, how they audition for their parts, and how they either perform successfully or fail to engage their audience from the minute they clock in in the morning to the time they clock out at night. We will delve into the business and professional performer's interaction with his or her superiors and their associates, and discover how this behavior mirrors the interfacing that a director and producer have with their fellow actors and actresses. We will see how these performances dictate success or failure in the business and professional worlds.

DISCOVER

- Why there are no insignificant employees in any organization

- Why most business start-ups fail ... and what to do about it

- The number-one role roadblock that business and professional performers face day to day

- How managing differs from leading

LET THE SHOW BEGIN

You are the Producer, Director, Actor and Choreographer in your performance. Your scripts, rehearsals and cast of characters are crucial to accomplishing the outcomes you desire.

It's about connecting at the emotional level vs. the intellectual level that will drive the shift in thinking of your audience.

In addition, it is imperative that you be authentic in your performance and believe in the value of the message you are conveying.

PATIENCE AND CARING

The same holds true in your personal life and in your relationships. When you understand the emotional drivers— I'm referring here to patience and caring—then your chances for a success increase manifold.

The one thing I'm sure of is that you can't have a loving relationship if you don't have a caring relationship. I also know that a display of impatience is often a sign of disrespect for your significant other, for your kids, for your friends, for your associates in the community. Patience and caring are the keys in every aspect of your life. And

> "People don't care what you know until they know that you care."
> BERNIE CRONIN

I will also tell you this; In my theater experience, the best performers care immensely about the roles they play and they care immensely about giving their audience the best performance they possibly can.

Here's something I hear all the time on the client development front: "Bernie, once I get in front of a qualified prospect I can close 80 percent of the time.

No kidding! That's not the problem; the problem is getting in front of them in the first place. I have conducted One-Day Boot Camps all over the United States. One of the things we do is make actual live calls on a speakerphone in front of all the attendees. You talk about fear and pressure! I make the first calls to kind of break the ice, but it's extremely difficult for others to step up in front of an audience of people they don't know and call a prospective stranger who might be a prospect for the products or services they sell.

One of my attendees once came up to me at the end of the session and said, "Bernie, when you were making that call, I was so nervous I thought I might get sick." I said to myself, "He's nervous and isn't even making the call." I later found out he was no longer employed by my client company. I felt bad for him, but clearly the client development arena was not for him.

A colleague of mine has an interesting parameter in helping his clients hire client developers. I once asked him, "What criteria do you use in hiring client developers associate for your organization?" Pretty simple, right?

He responded without hesitation, saying, "Bernie, the first thing I ask myself is would she/he make a good bartender?

Can they connect? Can they look you in the eye and make you feel confident that making and serving your drink is going to be a pleasurable experience?"

Wow! How many times since then have I asked myself that same question? Ever since, I have been teaching the owners and managers in my monthly Owners/Managers Leadership Forum Seminars to ask themselves the very same question.

What does this simple observation illustrate? It illustrates the fact that we most often "hire for skills and fire for attitude." Okay, so what does this have to do with being a good bartender? It tells us that the attitude someone brings to a job is far more important than if they know how to mix the right martini. First and foremost, you have to know how to connect. Making a martini is easy; you can learn that. Connecting comes from inside. You have to *want* to connect.

> "**Everything in the world we want to do and get done, we must do with and through people.**"
>
> EARL NIGHTINGALE

Bruce Springsteen has a technique for immediately connecting with his concert audiences. He gets copies of local newspapers and listens to local radio stations in the cities in which he is appearing and learns about what is happening locally in those cities, events that he can acknowledge and relate to in the art of connecting. When he travels to foreign countries he will learn about common phrases and salutations and greet his audience with his hello in their native tongue. Think they feel connected? Bet your life they do.

Malcolm Gladwell, in his bestselling book *The Tipping Point*, refers to people who know and connect others as "Connectors."

FIRST CONNECT

In my world of business development coaching, connectedness is most challenged when we talk about money and dealing with sticker shock. As Warren Buffett says, "Price is what you pay; value is what you get."

Another problem is presenting your solution too soon. I call it "Premature Pitchulation." So how much do you show your prospect? Here's my list: Make sure they get to see everything that relates to the pain you're trying to alleviate or end.

- If you have some bells and whistles that may help your cause, don't be afraid to show them to the prospect.

- Whenever possible, let the prospect make a tangible connection with the product. Let him see and touch it.

- If the prospect interrupts, stop presenting, no matter where you are. Stop and just listen. He or she is buying!

- You don't have to finish the presentation if you've found a prospect that turns into a buyer.

- Make your presentation in the prospect's preferred mode of taking in information, whatever that is: visual, auditory, or kinesthetic.

- Don't be afraid to abort.

AUTHENTICITY IS THE KEY

People understand Emotional Drivers (Subconsciously). I understand Emotional Drivers. In client development we relieve Emotional Displeasure.

One time, I had a crack across the windshield of my car. It drove me crazy. So one day, my wife got sick of me complaining. She received a phone prospecting call from an auto glass guy and then handed me the phone. She said, "The guy on the line is from Manhattan Auto Glass. He says he can fix the window so you'll stop bitching." I took the receiver and said,

"Hello."

He said, "Is it Mr. Cronin or Bernie?"

I liked that he asked. "Bernie is okay."

"This is Fred. I understand you've got a problem with your window."

"Yes."

"Well, here's what we need to do."

He used the power word "we." I liked that too.

"We need your office address. We need your insurance company. We'll do everything and you don't have to pay us any money. We'll file the claim for you. We're bonded. How does that sound?"

"It sounds great, Fred," I said. "But before we get off the phone, tell me how many calls you have to make before you find someone like me?"

"Sixty-four."

Fred found me when I was in pain, and he closed me. Find the person in pain. Fred's job was to stay uninvolved emotionally, but to get me emotionally involved. I know one thing; he clearly enjoyed the role he was playing, and I liked that about him too.

As I always say, "You're not getting out alive so you might as well have some fun along the way."

If you are having fun, the prospect understands that, because he or she also wants to have fun. I say in my training, "If you're not laughing, you're not learning." Laughter is infectious, especially if you make a joke about yourself. I train our people to watch *Columbo* episodes. Take on the detective role that Peter Falk played and act a little confused.

> "Most people spend more time and energy going around problems than trying to solve them."
>
> BERNIE CRONIN

As Eric Morris says, "You become the character. The character doesn't become you."

You should act from the inside out—from the emotions of the character you're playing, not from externals, like how the character is dressed.

Authenticity is the key. It is the key to the CEO playing her role in front of her C-level team. It is the key to the manager on the factory floor. It is the key to the man and the woman discussing their household budget. Yes, these are all roles

> "Acting is about becoming the character whose role you are performing. It is not about being something you are not."
>
> BERNIE CRONIN

we play. The CEO will go to the gym later that day and take on the role of a woman trying to stay fit. The factory floor manager will go out for a beer with his buddies after closing down the shop and take on the role of guy bonding with his friends. The man and woman will go into their toddler's bedroom after their budget discussion and take on the role of loving parents.

In my work, I've found that only about 5 percent of people are real leaders. Leaders deal with vision, and managers deal with complexities. There are a lot of managers out there, but not a lot of true leaders—and companies fail due to a lack of leadership. I believe that most leaders were once great followers of other leaders and learned the principles of leadership along the way.

Most people manage the way they were managed. If they were managed by a good leader, then they become good leaders. If they were managed by a poor leader, then they'll probably replicate what they learned and became poor managers and leaders themselves.

All relationships have this learning component built into them. We're creatures of imitation. If you associate with good and talented people, then your odds of being good and talented increase exponentially.

This is life. This is leadership. Being authentic in your roles brings each to life and takes your performance to the next level.

MANY SIDES OF CLIENT DEVELOPMENT PERFORMING

You don't have to be making cold calls from behind a desk, in the boardroom setting strategy, or on the factory floor managing the troops to be recognized as a business performer. You can be the person doing the buying. You can be the prospect listening to a pitch. You still have a role to play. You still have to perform.

Here's an example. One time I was buying a car for my wife up in Gloucester, Massachusetts. It was March 31, 2006. I walked into the dealership. I asked for the owner, because he and I were acquaintances, but he wasn't in. No problem. There were two reps in the showroom along with manager. It was four in the afternoon. It was dark outside and lightly snowing. My timing was no coincidence. It was all part of setting the stage and priming my audience.

I walked up to one of the reps, pointed to the car lot, and casually said, "I don't suppose all those cars out there are sold, are they?"

You can imagine his reaction. He said, "No. No, they're not." "Well, I might be interested in buying one."

We took a seat at his desk. Two doors down was his manager. We began talking about features and benefits and such and then moved on to price.

"I'm interested in that Infiniti out there," I said. I told him the model. "Are you ready?"'

"What do you mean?"

"Are you ready to close? You're only entitled to one trip to your manager. Two trips down there, and it's over."

You know how the rep's like to run back and forth to their managers, but I took that option away.

I threw out my price. He threw out his. Then he went to his manager. They chatted. He came back. He met my price, and we closed. I bought my car and signed off on it. I had a system and a methodology from the moment I came into the dealership. Who was in charge? I was.

It's the same thing for the CEO in the C-Suite. It's the same thing with the manager roaming the factory floor. It's the same in a client presentation. You must have a system and methodology that puts you in charge, even if the person sitting across from you doesn't know it.

The same holds true in the roles we assume as leaders and in life in general. As a leader, you have to be in charge. Of course, you also want your team to take ownership of their roles in the organization, to be proud of their roles and to be receptive to the directions you give.

> "If you find enough emotion, they will close themselves; that's why we say if there is no emotion, there's no change."

In the community, you want people to take action, but you want them to think that the decision to take action is theirs. No one wants to be ordered around or to be browbeaten. A good leader knows this.

HE WHO HESITATES

Charlie Anderson, a longtime friend and associate, and I were visiting a client in Somerville, Massachusetts, some years back.

The company's expertise was color-coding for hospital records. They were looking to expand and seriously exploring the possibility of a client development program for their employees. Bill, the company president, and Dave, his manager, listened to our entire presentation.

At the end of our pitch, I got right to the point and said, "Bill, what would you like to do now?"

"Well, I'm really interested," he said. I took his temperature and he said, "I'm close to a 10 but I want to think it over."

"That's not an option," I said simply. "I don't have a problem with a yes or a no, but anywhere in between doesn't work."

"What? Thinking about it is not an option?"

"No."

He looked at me and then he looked across at Dave and said, "Dave, what do you think?"

"I like it," Dave said.

Bill said, "All right, let's go."

Charlie and I got to the car after closing the deal and nearly peed in our pants, we were laughing so hard.

"Bill, I'm sorry, but that's not an option," I repeated. "And it worked!" Charlie said.

But the point was that Charlie and I had found Bill's emotional driver. His company needed more business and needed it desperately. Their people weren't performing, and we had a solution.

Charlie Anderson didn't always work for me. He was someone who wanted to run his own show and be the producer and director of it. I respected that.

But for two years prior to our association, he would come to me on a regular basis and say, "Bernie, I want to come to work with you."

"I can't hire you, Charlie," I told him more than once. "I've got no salary to pay you and not enough customers for both of us. I've got no benefits and you've got three kids at home and a wife."

"I want to do it. I've got a little set aside, I can do it."

He wanted to put together his own client list, and I had the connections to help him do this. I also had a system and a methodology that maximized performance, and Charlie was smart enough to make it work for him. We finally agreed to give it a try. The first month he made 410 dials and had something like $12,000 in business. Each call was worth about $33. The next month he got up to $47 per call. Pretty soon Charlie was seriously kicking ass, and I was glad we had come to terms.

Along the way, Charlie created a system of his own. He would look at *The Boston Globe* on Sundays for companies that were hiring and then he'd call and say, "If you are hiring, you're going to need a trainer." He did very well. Then he landed a big client down in Greenwich, Connecticut, called World Color, one of the largest printing companies in the world. Eventually, they hired him away from me, but they did so with my blessing. And then he went on his own and opened his own coaching business and authored two books, one with well-known author Brian Tracy.

What made Charlie great was that he had a lot of guts and could reach out to anybody on the phone. He wasn't particularly outgoing or personable at social gatherings, but he could sell. His philosophy was simple: "I'll do whatever it takes to get the business."

As shy as he may have been outside of work, he was equally as fearless when it came to making calls. He knew how to play that role better than anyone else. He knew how to flip the switch and become a consummate business performer.

A lot of actors are like Charlie. They're basically shy and introverted. Take Harrison Ford. He doesn't hold press conferences. He doesn't go on television. You never see him.

Billy Crystal is another good example. He is not a real outgoing kind of guy. I know Billy because his brother lives across the street from us. Billy comes to visit him and spends a few hours every day at our pool. He doesn't congregate. He finds a spot at one end of the pool and relaxes. He's a nice guy but he's not the gregarious figure we see him playing in a number of his movies.

I think that many of these actors enjoy playing roles where they can be somebody they are not and never will be. It's always fascinating when people dress up for Halloween. For that one night, they can be whatever or whoever they want. I think that applies to a lot of people in the theater and also to a lot of people in business. It's the role that's important when you're working, and working it makes you a great performer.

We all act all of the time. Sometimes, I'll say to myself, "I have to go to this %$#@* networking meeting, and I really don't want to. But, I really should be there."

So I'll put on my meeting persona and go and be what I need to be for those two hours. I'll play the role. I'll perform. I have fun with it. Then I get the hell out of there. I return home and slip into the role of husband, dad, and relaxed Red Sox fan.

The best business performers know they have a role to play. Actually, more than one role. The CEO has one persona when he is meeting with his team. He takes on another persona when he stands in front of the board of directors. He goes out and plays golf with potential clients and falls into still a third role.

You have a role that serves you in front of your superiors. You put on a completely different air when you meet with your peers. And then when you step onto the factory floor, you assume the roles of a supervisor, manager, and mentor.

The best advice I can give you is to embrace each of your roles. This begins by recognizing each and every role. Know your scripts. Know your fellow actors. Know your audience. Then step out on stage and break a leg!

CURTAIN CALL

The best business performers know they have many roles to play, and they understand how much it helps to have a system that supports those roles.

People skills are a science that the best business performers never tire of studying.

A good leader knows that no one likes to be ordered around or browbeaten, and he or she makes sure every performance has a positive note to it.

In the end, every role the business performer assumes is about connecting.

OUT OF THE BOX OFFICE:
(BERNIE'S PERSONAL CHALLENGE)

"NOTIVATION... go for No." In addition to *yes* Goals in business and life you need to set *no* Goals. In business, 60 percent of all customers say NO before saying YE$. My colleague, Andrea Waltz from www.goforno.com says, "You can have virtually anything you want if you're willing to hear no often enough and that yes is the destination and no is how you get there." Please visit her site for more: www.goforno.com.

"The restaurant business is like being on stage on Broadway, only we do matinees daily."

ELLA BRENNAN, BRENNAN'S OF NEW ORLEANS

ACT 5

ROLES OF THE PRODUCER AND DIRECTOR

PLAYBILL

In Act 5, Roles of the Producer and Director, we will discuss not only the roles of the Producer and Director as they pertain to the theater and how they are key components in putting on an exceptional play, but we will also discuss how we take on the roles of a producer and director in our daily lives. We will explore the roles of the producer and director at the C-Suite level. We will examine how the best leaders are, in many ways, both the producers and directors within their own companies, men and women who know how to meld purpose, motivation, and direction into every role they assume.

DISCOVER

- How each of us is the producer and director of our own lives

- How to produce and direct in any leadership roles you might undertake

- When the best time to produce is and when the best time to direct is

- How cultural alignment plays into the role of producing and directing

LET THE SHOW BEGIN

It has been said that, "Playwriting is storytelling."

Playwriting has also been described as, "Words thrown out into the emptiness of space in search of a response."

That's where the producer and director come into the picture. It is all well and good to throw words out into the emptiness of space, but things only really get interesting when someone makes sense of those words (the director) and someone puts together a production worthy of an audience (the producer).

At age 82, actor/director Clint Eastwood staged a talk at the Tribeca Film Festival following a screening of Richard Schickel's documentary titled *Eastwood Directs: The Untold Story.*

Eastwood regaled the Tribeca Performing Arts Center with the accrued, pragmatic wisdom accumulated during his long and illustrious career as a filmmaker.

He began by expressing admiration for the 104-year-old Portuguese director Manoel de Oliveira. "It would be great to be 105 and still making films," Eastwood said, "even if that does make me the ultimate optimist."

Some of the highlights from the Tribeca talk stuck with me as appropriate for our chapter on the roles of the director and producer, and I've shared them here:

On preferring to begin a take with: "Go when you're ready," rather than the traditional "Action!" Eastwood said, "Action puts a bad connotation out there, like some firecracker that goes off to get everyone going."

On his willingness to take suggestions for a scene from anyone: "You have to steal a lot. You have to have a criminal mentality to be a film director."

On the role of the director in a film production: "A lot of people have fallen in love with the authoritarian theory, but the truth is, you're merely a Platoon Captain."

On the studio executives who told him no one would want to see a film about women boxing (the best-picture winning *Million Dollar Baby*): "Who the hell wants to see anything? You never know until you get into it."

The reason I started this section with the Clint Eastwood story is that he has played all the parts. He's been an actor, he's been a producer, and he has been a director at the top level. And whether we're talking about business, leadership, or life in general, you need to understand all the different roles you're certain to be playing as well as those taken on by everyone around you. Once you understand the roles and how they fit into one cohesive unit, you can become the director of your own play in whatever area of your life you choose.

The last thing you and I want to do is abdicate our roles as director or producer to somebody else, especially in our own personal lives. This is not to say that we don't learn from others, or that we don't need mentors or teachers. We do. And we also need people in our lives that we can confidently assign a task and know it's going to be done correctly. Producers and directors don't do everything. They find the best people for any particular job, and then let them run with it.

THEATER AND LIFE: A MIRROR REFLECTION

Which reminds me of a question I ask in all my Keynote Addresses: Does acting imitate entrepreneurship or does entrepreneurship imitate acting?

Here's a hint for you. Both entrepreneurship and acting contain seven key elements. Let's explore them:

Number one: Believing. Do you believe in your acting? By the same token, do you believe in your product, your service, your team?

Number two: Focus. Can you totally focus on your acting every single time, consistently, and with confidence? Likewise, can you focus 100 percent of your energy on that client development interview, that board meeting, that brainstorming session?

Number three: Are you zoomed in? When you develop a strong memory of the role you're playing, it then feels effortless. When you believe in your business approach, it just happens.

Number four: Au naturel. Can you put your acting on autopilot? Can you walk into a business presentation so prepared that each word has a purpose?

Number five: Do you stay in control? Do you feel in control of your acting as well as your role? Do you allow your prospective client to feel as in control of your business presentation while you continue to guide the process exactly where you want it to go?

Number six: Are you thinking clearly? Do you think about what your next move will be and where you want to go, or do you just stand and deliver lines? Are you one step ahead of your business client, or are you just winging it?

Number seven: Can you have fun? Let's face it, when

you play well it is fun, whether you're on the boards or in the boardroom.

IT'S ALL ABOUT RESULTS

On some level, everything we do results in some change, some growth, some evolution, some shift in thinking, as Charlie Anderson explores in his book "*SHIFT THINKING*" and Mark Bonchek directs in his "*SHIFT ACADEMY*". In the theater, the result the producer and director are hoping to inspire is a powerful response from the audience. That is the goal. The goal is one person telling another person they have to go see this play; it's wonderful, or moving, or hilarious. A strong review will likely lead to a long run, whether it's on Broadway or in a local theater in Buffalo.

> "Guts and Humor are the two most important ingredients in business. You have to have some fun with it. That's part of your theater, your show."
>
> BERNIE CRONIN

In the business world, the result you're looking for is profit. Profit suggests a product or service that people desire. Positive referrals lead to more business. Now your direction is paying off. As a producer, your strategy is bearing fruit.

In both cases, you're keeping your doors open, staying afloat, and prospering.

In the real world, strong relationships are the result of taking charge of your own life and being yourself. As the producer of your own play, you feel good about yourself. You accept your own flaws and revel in your strengths. Those are some pretty darn good results.

It takes guts to be a director. It takes guts to be a producer. It doesn't matter whether you are talking about your own life, whether you are talking about the boardroom, or whether you are talking about a one-man show on Main Street; you must have guts and you must have humor.

THINK IT OVER (TIO)

If you're the director or producer of your own show — I'm talking "big picture" show, a man who owns his own business, a woman seeking financing for her new start-up, or a CEO drumming up support for a new program with his board of directors—then the only result you *don't* want to hear is "TIO." What is TIO? Think it over. "Give me a week. I'll think it over." "I like where you're going with this, but I want to think it over." You get the picture. We've all heard it.

But whether it's a new business call, or a kid calling the prettiest girl in his class for a date, the last thing you want to hear is "Think it over." Why? Because TIO means "no."

Hearing "no" is good. "No" is no problem. You say thank you very much and move on. If you hear "Think it over," do the very same thing. Get rid of that prospect and find another one.

If a producer is looking for a company to finance his play or a theater to house his play, he'd rather hear, "It's not going to work," than, "Let me think it over."

When I hear a client say, "I'll think it over," I say, "Sorry, that's not an option. Yes is an option. So is no. TIO is not an option."

If a director approaches an actor with a part, and she says, "Listen, let me give it some thought," my advice would be, find yourself another girl. There are plenty out there dying for the part.

CONGRATULATIONS

Remember this: when you see yourself as the director or the producer of your own show, whether it's in life, business, or in the theater, your world revolves around decision making. Decisions require a commitment to action, and the one thing every producer and director advocates for is people taking action. Movement. Energy. Jumping into the parade with both feet. Now you're getting things done.

People love to be congratulated.

Then we say to them, "The original investment deposit is $5,000. How do you plan to pay for this? A check, credit card, wire transfer?" If they say, "Can you do automatic checking (ACH)?" I say, "You bet your life I can."

That check goes into my account the same day. No sweat.

This is the moment where you've set the stage to ask for a referral.

First you say, "We'll get all this delivered." Then you add, "If you're satisfied, I'm going to ask for three referrals of similar people who'd be interested in making a donation. Would you be okay with that?"

> "Fifty percent of referrals turn into business. If you get enough referrals, you'll be fine. Remember, everybody knows 250 people."

You want to get their validation. If you earned the right to ask and have done a good enough job, they'll say yes. Sometimes people worry about what you're going to do with the referrals you got from them. So you tell them "all I'm going to do is call your referral and introduce myself and see if there's a fit. Then I'll call you back and tell you what happened. I'll let you know if they're interested or not."

BELIEF: THE MAGIC WORD

If people won't invest or take action or jump in the parade, blame it on belief—or the lack thereof. That's the magic word—belief. It always goes back to belief.

In business, if you're not sure that the decision maker believes in your product, go back and revisit him.

Always remember: *buyers are liars.* So when you ask someone who makes the decisions and they say, "I do," the important thing to remember is that is usually a lie.

In my way of thinking, you always ask, "Who else besides you would be involved in this decision?"

Using an analogy that all directors and producers understand, I like to learn who their cast of characters is. Who has the leading role? Who is the supporting actor? Who has a bit part?

Just like in the movie *Jerry Maguire,* actor Cuba Gooding, Jr., if you recall, was the football player Rod Tidwell. But Rod wasn't the decision maker in the family. That role belonged to his wife. She said to her husband, "You are not going to sign with that other agent. We're going to go with Jerry." Tom Cruise knew she was the decision maker and used that influence to close the deal.

Here's a communication hint that all directors and producers of note never forget. No matter whom you're talking to, use their preferred method of communication: visual, auditory, or kinesthetic. Match your prospect's posture, body movement, rate of speech, tone, favorite phrases, and handshake. Every good director knows this.

I coach people that 72 percent of the time they will get a voicemail from someone rather than connecting directly. When you return the call and leave your own voicemail message, match and mirror their tonality, their cadence, and their inflection. That's how to get return calls. And always dress the part for the role you're playing, with the right costume.

With a bank group, for instance, I always play the part of the producer and wear a white shirt. I trained 50 people at Bank United, the largest bank in Florida. There were 50 people there, 20 women and 30 men, and 24 of the men had on white shirts. I bonded and "bankered" with them through my shirt. Insurance people wear their jackets in the office, with ties. Colored shirts are okay with them. Good acting stuff. Take the time to learn certain key phrases that people use in their business and then match them. (This is an old producer trick.) I once knew a guy who ran the wealth management division for Bank of America. He told me, "Our people are just not digging down enough. They don't get enough wallet share," which means that they may have $5 million under management, but they aren't getting the other $10 or $20 million of their clients' assets.

I was driving when I heard this and immediately pulled over to the side of the road and wrote down, "wallet share."

I met with the man two weeks later and he said, "Tell me what you think about our business."

I calmly replied, "I usually find that wealth management people don't get enough wallet share."

"Finally," he said, "I found somebody who gets it!" Talk about a director at work. Know how to inspire your actors.

Know your audience. Use buzz words to your benefit. Part of being a director is knowing the parlance of your particular industry. It's also about crafting your language to fit your audience; are you talking to your board of directors, your management team, or the guys on the factory floor? Make sure you know your audience. The producer in a play has to know the audience he and his team are targeting. This influences the set, the costumes, the pricing. The CEO in her role as a producer has to be prepared to set the goals of her company, create strategy to meet those goals, and then understand the tactics her team needs to get there. As the director, she has to know how to motivate her team and give the kind of guidance they will need in moving forward.

BELIEVE IN YOU

You've got to be sincere about the product or service you're providing to your clients, whether you're in the theater or in the business world. You can't represent something you don't truly believe in—so you must become your own first and best customer.

When I started out one of my colleagues told me, "The first thing you should do is join your own training program."

I thought about this and then wrote a check for $5,000 to sign up for the program. Of course, it went into my account, but I went through the motions of writing a check and becoming a client of myself. I filled out a form and signed it as the owner of the company. Then I said, "Hey, I put money in this company. I believe in this."

Here's a poignant example of scripting. Very powerful. Jan is a client of mine. One day she called me to discuss a very real, very typical dilemma.

She'd been invited to a meeting with a big bank headquartered out of Alabama, but the meeting got cancelled and her contact at the bank wouldn't return her e-mails or calls.

"What should I do?" she asked me.

I play-acted the roles for her, and said, "Go to the bank and walk into this man's office and ask if he's there."

"Walk into his office? What if he's not there?"

"Then leave a card that says, 'Sorry I missed you. Here's my cell phone. Call me.'"

"What about his secretary?" "Less is more. Don't tell her a lot. Just tell her you were invited to a meeting with the man and you just want to meet him."

"What if he's there?"

"Sit down and spend a couple of minutes. Ask him when we are going to reschedule our meeting. And how many people will be there so I'll know how many handouts to bring."

"What if his secretary says, 'Is he expecting you?'" "You say, 'I certainly hope so.'"

"Will he think that's too aggressive?"

"I don't know what he'll think. He may think you're assertive. He may also think you're passionate enough to be someone he should listen to. He may be testing you to see how passionate you are."

I prepared Jan for her role, but she was nervous as hell walking into the bank to meet this man. She left her card with the secretary, but without coaching, she wouldn't have done this. Like an actor, she needed to lose herself in the role she was playing that day. She detached herself from her own emotions and portrayed the emotions of the character she was in at that moment—be it angry, sad, glad, happy, jovial or whatever other feelings were called for. You take on the role of businessperson and set yourself aside, exactly as an actor does.

I coach people to make cold calls. I show how to interrupt a secretary's patterns. I'll call someone and say, "It's Bernie for Bob. Is he in?"

I've broken her habit of saying, "Who's calling," because I've already told her that.

> "Talent is overrated. We work to become a successful person and we practice and we rehearse. We learn to do something over and over, until it becomes natural."
>
> BERNIE CRONIN

The typical business person says, "May I speak with Bob?" "Who is calling?"

"Bernie."

"What's this about?"

This is where you don't want to be. Instead, announce

yourself and ask if Bob is in, knowing she now has to answer a direct question. "Yes, he is."

Then I say, "Can you put me through?" She's off balance because you kept her off balance. That's the theater part of it.

Sometimes, a secretary might hang up on you. If that happens, I call back and say, "We got disconnected." These are the techniques we practice In my acting boot camps. We make live calls and it's a hoot. Vince Lombardi said, "The key to the success of the Green Bay Packers was repetition, repetition, repetition."

CURTAIN CALL

Know the seven most important words in closing a business deal: "What would you like to do now?"

Your job as a producer or director is to get people to make a decision, take action, and be inspired.

Thinking it over is not an option.

No one will invest in your vision if you aren't fully invested yourself.

OUT OF THE BOX OFFICE
(BERNIE'S PERSONAL CHALLENGE)

Don't Practice ... have a RECITAL!

The next time you have a major business interview or presentation or address to a group or committee, I challenge you to prepare and rehearse your scene. Then enlist the help of colleagues to be your audience and role-play the scenario. You be the playwright and spell out the roles, concerns, emotional drivers, etc., and then recite the scene. It will change your life.

> "The mother of skill is repetition."
> TONY ROBBINS

ACT 6

ROLES OF THE EXECUTIVES AND MANAGERS

PLAYBILL

In Act 6, *Roles of the Executives and Managers*, we will explore how the men and women who have risen to Leadership positions in their companies, big or small, take on roles that change with each level of their activity, and continue to change based on the people they deal with, who they answer to, who answers to them, and the strategies and tactics that drive their goals. Whether you work for yourself or whether you work for a Fortune 500 company, we will discuss just how these various roles require nuances that can dictate your success or failure moving forward.

DISCOVER

- How the roles of the Executives and Managers relate to one another

- How to avoid conflict in these roles

- How to recognize top performers at the Executive/Manager level

- How to become a top performer at the Executive/Manager level

LET THE SHOW BEGIN

My biggest discoveries came early in my career when I learned how to speak effectively in front of groups of all shapes and sizes. Most important to this learning process was an understanding of precisely who the audience was at any given time. When you're in the Leadership Suite, you will likely face a variety of audiences during the course of any given day, and you will have to change your delivery to fit the occasion, much like actors do based on the type of play they are acting in and the type of audience they are expecting any given night. A CEO has to know the makeup of his/her team and play to it, just like a director has to be fully aware of the strengths and weaknesses of the actors at his or her disposal.

As I looked at the challenge of public speaking way back when, I kept thinking about the word "audience" and that brought to mind the theater. Producers, directors, writers, and actors have to know who their audience is. Are you playing a college or university campus with a group of young people, or are you playing on Broadway? What about off-Broadway? What about a neighborhood in-the-round or an outdoor amphitheater? Theater people must know where they are and what the makeup of their audience is, even the demographics. They are selling a product, their message; you can't sell a product if you don't understand the pros and cons of the people doing the buying.

COMMUNICATION AND CONNECTION

Theater people use many of the same techniques as Executive/Manager leaders, and Executive/Manager leaders use similar techniques as actors: tell them what you're going to tell them, tell them, and then tell them what you just told them.

It's all about communication and connection, and you won't be any more successful in business than you are in the theater if you can't connect and communicate. Oh, and try having a relationship without those skills. Not likely.

In theater, you have a show title; this gives a sense of what the audience is going to see on stage. You have a program that expands on the theme. And then you keep building on that theme throughout the presentation, act after act. The

> " The best leaders, almost without exception and at every level, are master users of stories and symbols. "
>
> TOM PETERS

viewers will absorb all this and walk away with a message or an image or an impression. Obviously, you want them to have a positive experience so they will return to the theater again, just like the businessman wants to create a positive experience that will garner the loyalty of his clients and their willingness to advocate for his company.

If you're a business leader, you want to generate the kind of environment that breeds loyalty among your team and organization, and you also want everyone in your organization to advocate for the success of your business. You want the same thing from your customers.

The more I thought about this dynamic, the more I realized that in business the goal is the same: You want your prospect to take action and buy something. In *Death of a Salesman*, Arthur Miller wants his audience to know that salesman Willie Loman suffers from a very high need for approval. He wants his audience to come away from the play knowing that Willie was unsuccessful primarily because he always wanted to be liked, as opposed to respected. We react to him on stage and we never forget him because he touches our emotions so deeply. We all want approval in some way, but you have to be careful how you go about getting it.

The C-Suite, however, is a little different. Being liked is not a prerequisite for the Executive/Manager. However, being respected in the C-Suite is. In the C-Suite, we are not looking for approval. We are setting strategy, and we are expecting people to acknowledge that strategy. However, it gets a little more complicated than that. You need your team to buy into your strategy and your purpose. You want them to take the direction that you give and run with it. You want to be able to motivate your people. These all require the nuances of role-playing.

When you are in the C-Suite you are not worried about being liked. You are not looking for approval. You want your actions to garner respect. You want your actions to garner action. When a strategy is set, you expect the people who report to you to implement the tactics. We are not expecting them to cheer or clap, just do the job. But again, you understand that the more your team takes ownership of the company's goals and readily make them their own goals, the more effective they will be in their jobs. The best leaders in the C-Suite create an environment where a job isn't just seen as a job, but as a calling. A good leader has to be many things to many different people, and he or she had better know how to change roles at a moment's notice.

The more I studied the theater, the more the parallel just kept coming back and jumping out at me. You've got to be a showman, and you've got to connect with people's emotions in order to make the deepest impression. You've got to make people "feel" when you're in front of them.

Prominent author, management theorist, and college president Warren Bennis, in his 1989 book titled *On Becoming a Leader,* provides many insights, and perhaps the key one, and a mighty theme of the book, is this: "True leaders are not interested in proving themselves; they want above all to be able to express themselves fully."

ONE SIZE DOES NOT FIT ALL

In the C-Suite, training, coaching, and mentoring are more important than supervising. Most people don't quit companies, they quit bosses.

It is important in the C-Suite level that you don't manage and lead every person the same way. Different teammates require different motivators. Some need honey and some need vinegar.

Just as in the theater, a director directs each actor individually. Yes, they are putting together a cohesive play, but each actor requires an individual set of motivators.

EXECUTIVE AND MANAGEMENT LEADERSHIP OF DIFFERENT GENERATIONS

With voice communications being a thing of the past, as the primary form, the ability to connect viscerally in order to convey an intended message is much more difficult and must be crafted for our audiences in one or more of the generational categories above.

For example, my best friend and grandson, 14 year-old Dillon, put on an Academy Award performance to invite his first date to a Homecoming Dance. So he became a playwright for his invitational scene using technology (text) and props.

He asked his mom, my daughter Sharon, to buy him a 3x2 foot white poster board and permanent markers. Once prepared for his scene, at 6 p.m. he boarded his bicycle with his poster board for the short trip to the home of his female invitee to the Homecoming Dance. He stopped his bike in full view of the front window and texted his classmate to come to the front window. Then he raised his poster board with the message: "HOMECOMING DANCE?"

After reading the message, she immediately texted Dillon her response: YES!

Note, not a word was spoken and only six words were texted: "Come to the front window" and "Yes."

In 2013, I was training a class of College Admissions Counselors and I suggested the value of a handwritten thank-you note, handwritten with a postage stamp and not a postage meter. One young lady questioned, "Why not just send an email or text thank-you? Why take the time, use paper, and waste 46 cents on a postage stamp?"

I was perplexed by her response and ready to challenge her, but then reminded myself of the most important rule in communicating and theater…know your audience!

Today's workforce at many companies is often made up of five different generations: Traditionalists, Baby Boomers, Gen X'ers, Gen Y'ers, and Millennials.

Gen Y'ers (dubbed Gen Why's) represent nearly a quarter of the workforce today and will be more than 50 percent by 2020. As a group, they are both ambitious and demanding—qualities that many boomers, eyeing retirement after years spent paying their dues and diligently moving up the ladder, find enraging. In addition, Y'ers are more technically competent and more comfortable with different ethnic and racial groups. They can also stand to learn a few things from their boomer forebears—like how to sell clients on a concept, earn their trust, and close a deal (a selling performance). There's also basic business protocol, such as what *not* to say or wear in a particular situation.

Further, a Payscale study (Payscale is a provider of compensation data and software) reports that 47 percent of the Gen Y workforce is opting for employment at smaller firms versus 23 percent who choose companies of more than 1,500 employees. Fortune 500 companies could be losing out on this valuable talent because of corporate cultures that dissuade employee input and collaboration from all employees. Gen Y'ers won't stick around long if they can't contribute to the bigger, broader corporate mission and vision.

When I studied at the Burt Reynolds of Film and Theater, I learned all I could about my characters before I played them: what they were like emotionally, where they grew up, what kind of families they came from, what their cultural and political bent was, their habits, their fears, their phobias. The idea was to uncover everything I could about my characters and the worlds they populated.

Believe me when I tell you that the best leaders know as much about the people they are managing, motivating, and directing as they possibly can, right down to the birthdays of their children, their favorite movies, and their worst fears. Now you've got the goods to get people to take action and go that extra mile for you.

> "You don't stop laughing because you grow old. You grow old because you stop laughing."
>
> GEORGE BERNARD SHAW

> # "Make a client; not a sale."
> ## BERNIE CRONIN

A lot of times in business, you don't know to whom you will be talking on any particular business, but you can find out what you need to know through the "interview." I never use the word "business call." I always use the word "interview," as if I were a news reporter approaching a journalistic assignment. Which reminds me: I think journalism would be a great training ground for business, leadership, and love.

Remember, however, that while the interview is important, it is only part of the show. What the other person says is just as important, if not more. You and your prospective client are both actors in the same scene. The better you know your part, the better you can respond to his (or her) part.

The old backslapping *Music Man* type of promoting is becoming much less prevalent today. Now it's more about team performances. I might meet with a CFO, a CIO, and perhaps a CEO. In any case, it is incumbent upon me to do my due diligence so that my theatrical troop is in sync with my audience.

HE WHO OVER-PREPARES

Another thing I discovered in my many years in the business world is that sometimes you can actually be over-prepared for a job. Whether it's in business, in pursuing a relationship, or even in the C-Suite, over-preparation stalls your momentum. Some people waste too much time preparing and it prejudges their decision. Sometimes, less is more.

When you're a businessman, sometimes, you want to know a little bit about a business, but not too much.

An example of this from my experience is a company like General Dynamics. You could study the corporate headquarters and their mission statement, but you'll just be meeting with one of the divisions. You look at that division and look at all their people. You study their LinkedIn profiles. You read their bios. You've spent all this time, but in reality you're still only meeting with one guy. He's the one you really need to know something about. Over-preparing can cloud your objectivity, especially at a first meeting, because you go in there with a lot of preconceived ideas. You don't need to know that much—and you always need to be able to improvise, just like in the theater.

The best guys (and gals) at the C-Suite level are the guys and gals who know how to wing it when they have to. They can be themselves in any setting, and yet they also know that every setting calls for a different role.

At a first meeting, all you're working on is trust and relationship. All you're trying to do is get a second meeting. I call it "Scene Building." The first scene is getting the first meeting. The second scene might be meeting with their staff. The third scene might be a proposal. The fourth scene might be delivering a proposal. The fifth scene might be giving them a taste of what we can do for one of their teams. Today, most of us are not in the one-meeting business. We're in the relationship business. A C-Suite leader's most important job is assembling a cohesive team that can work in harmony. In most cases, there is no place on a team for Lone Rangers. They can be disruptive, they can obstruct continuity, and they can hurt morale. Even in the theater, the lead actor must work in conjunction with his or her supporting actors, with the entire cast, or the lack of continuity and disharmony will show the moment they step onto the stage.

THE BUSINESS OF ART

Just as leaders at all levels of business can learn from producers and directors about teambuilding, so should actors, director, and producers have a pulse on the business world as well. The two are not separate. We live in a capitalistic society. Opportunities come and go. You can't live in a bubble. Art and business are not separate, no matter how idealistic you might be. Know both worlds so then you can use both worlds.

In December 2007, a writers strike shut down theater productions all over New York City and acting work dried up in, dare I say, a New York minute. It was not pretty. Many actors were forced to take holiday related jobs. They wrapped packages, addressed cards, and played Santa Claus, doing anything they could find to make ends meet. These weren't stars; these were actors who took roles on soap operas, in commercials, in off-Broadway productions, anything to pay the bills. Ironically, there was an upside to these odd jobs. Each job was, in essence, a character study. Every

> ## "There's no traffic jam on the extra mile."
> ### ZIG ZIGLAR

shopper, every retail employee, every person offered a chance to observe, study, learn, and interact.

During this time, one employment agency owner told *The New York Times*, "Actors make excellent temps because they're very enjoyable and have flexible schedules. They do well in corporate jobs as well because they can sell the role. They can be whatever you want them to be in any office setting. They can rise to any occasion."

Likewise, in April 2015, Tea Party of Miami and Florida Citizens Against Waste called for a demonstration against an Everglades land buying proposal by the South Florida Water Management District. Where do you find demonstrators, you ask? The answer is you post an acting opportunity on the Facebook page of the Broward Acting Group to become a protester, hold signs and chant "Stop The Waste" and "Stop The Land Grab" for the daily fee of $75. More than 50 actors sought the 40 person protesting group to stand behind a fence holding banners and signs while chanting.

Directors, producers, and actors are in a strange business. These are people who see an opportunity and grab it. They don't have the luxury of picking and choosing. They want to work, and they know any opportunity might never come again. The same is true in *the business world.*

Opportunity doesn't always have a pretty face. Sometimes it comes in the form of an obstacle, a detour, or a failure. You don't make it to the C-Suite without seizing every opportunity and fighting through every obstacle. You go the extra mile. You sacrifice. You take a risk.

In theater, you play the same role but to a different audience every night. Same for the C-Suite. A CEO doesn't deliver a message in the same way to every audience.

You learn as an actor to come from different places with each performance so you can deliver the playwright's message with the same power. This is also true in the business world. You sell to a new audience every day. I learn something from my clients every time we interact. One of them recently mentioned to me how he gets people to call him back and how he gets them to commit to meetings. When he leaves a meeting, he always asks, "When will it be appropriate for me to call you back?" That's a great choice of words. Not, "When can I call you or when should we talk?" but, "When will it be appropriate for me to call you back?"

I learned this from him and I use it.

Wayne Dyer tells the story of a Zen master who is visited by a professor from Harvard University. They're talking about Zen and the professor is babbling and saying this and that. The Zen master asks, "Would you like some tea?"

"Yes," the professor replies.

The Zen master gives him a teacup and he starts pouring and doesn't stop. The cup fills up and the tea spills all over the professor's pants.

"Master, master," the professor says, "the cup is full."

"That's your problem. You are too full and there's no room to put anything in." That's the metaphor Dyer used to support his point.

You should always have room within yourself to learn new things and to learn from everyone you meet.

KNOW YOUR ROLE OR DON'T AUDITION FOR IT

Here is a question that I'd like to ask every C-Level officer: Why do 75 percent of all department managers fail. Answer: Because they haven't been given the skill sets to recruit, interview, hire, train, grow, and mentor their people. Companies take a top performer and make him/her the manager. You just lost a good performer and created a manager with no proven skills at the position.

Take my word for it. There are many men and women in C-Suite positions who shouldn't be there either. They don't understand their roles. They don't have the skills of great directors and effective producers, people who know how to get the most out of other people.

You see this same thing all the time in sports. Ted Williams was a great ball player, but a lousy manager. Companies don't spend enough money investing in their C-Suite people. Why? It's crazy.

The selection process is so important. Some introverts succeed in positions requiring people skills in spite of themselves. I had a guy working for me once who was a member of Mensa. He was obnoxious in person, but great on the phone. He could really close business. Once he got in a role, strapped on his headset and dialed, he was totally in character and could he perform. Who knew?

Thomas International has studied more than 30,000 people in business development positions. They found:

- 8 percent of the people who have a good profile do not perform

- 2 percent who don't have a good profile do perform

- 38 percent of the people who have a good profile perform

- 52 percent who don't have a good profile don't perform. And yet people keep hiring the latter group even when they're not wired to prospect and close and generate new clients. It's a very difficult role to play every day.

Typically in insurance companies, only 20 percent of employees are still with the company after four years. That means 80 percent fail! Yet this doesn't seem to hurt the insurance companies. They hire the wrong people or they hire someone who can only sell to their mother, brother, sister, and uncles. Then they fire them, but everyone in the family keeps the policies. Whose names are on the tall buildings over the country? Insurance companies. Why? They take in more money than they pay out. It's a great model for success.

I wish I owned one of those companies.

As I said, I love the hunt in business. I love prospecting and turning that initial suspect into a prospect and then into a customer and eventually into a client. Clients will sell for you; they'll give you referrals and you won't

> "Why do they call it Life Insurance when you have to die to collect? Why don't they call it Death Insurance?"
> BERNIE CRONIN

167

have to make cold phone calls. They'll become your advocate. That's where you want to be, but it all starts with a prospect.

The best business people are like the best film directors. They understand the audition and selection process, and turning them into long-term clients who then send them referrals. Clint Eastwood is a good example, although he came up as an actor. Over decades, he's become a student of the whole film business. He understands where the screenwriter is coming from and he can look at a movie from the side of money and management—and from the point of view of the director, the producer or the actors. Some people love and enjoy a certain role and some people don't want to be more than actors. Jack Nicholson doesn't direct or produce. Ben Affleck and Matt Damon, like Eastwood, have grown into producers. The more you know about the business and the more skills you have, the more you can control. That's ultimately what actors, directors, and business people want.

A lot of people, in business and acting get into their comfort zone and want to stay there. Particularly in business, I find many people who have what I call an "incomestat." They make a certain amount of money and that's all they will ever make. They don't think or act like six-figure people. They believe they're going to stay at the level they are and they're comfortable in that position. They've reached their "incomestat" and they're satisfied.

You very rarely ever see anyone who's gotten to six

figures who ever went back below that level. Once they start to think like a six-figure income person, they act like one and continue making more money.

When I interview someone, I always ask, "What's the most money you've ever made in your life?"

They answer and then I ask, "How much have you averaged in the last three years?"

They answer that and then I say, "How much do you need to sustain your lifestyle?"

> # DAILY MANTRA:
> "I expand in abundance, success, and love every day, and inspire those around me to do the same."
> GAY HENDRICKS

If they tell me $75,000, that's probably all they're ever going to make. If they say, "I've got to make $150,000. I've got alimony, I've got the kids, I've got to do this and that. I've got to make $150,000 to $200,000."

That's the person I'm probably going to hire for a business development position.

C-Suite folks want to be top performers. They want to

have the lead role. They work hard, they audition hard, and they want to make the big bucks that come with it.

In the theater, some people are satisfied with the supporting role. They are satisfied with holding a backup role. C-Suite folks are the lead actors. They want the lead role. And they want what goes with it.

CURTAIN CALL

The best business people are like the best film directors. They understand hunting for prospects and turning them into long-term clients who then send them referrals.

Preparation is important, but over-preparation can ruin a good thing. Know when to say enough is enough.

Opportunity doesn't always have a pretty face. Sometimes it comes in the form of an obstacle, a detour, or a failure. Seize it anyway.

Life is no different than the boardroom or the stage. One size doesn't fit all.

OUT OF THE BOX OFFICE
(BERNIE'S PERSONAL CHALLENGE)

Leaders are readers.

I challenge you to read one hour per day in three 20 minute sessions in your world of interest. That will translate into one book per week, 52 books per year and 520 books in 10 years.

My Palm Beach, FL neighbor, Author James Patterson's major focus today is on promoting reading or, what he refers to as "our greatest endangered species."

ACT 7

THE AUDITION

PLAYBILL

> *In Act 7, The Audition, we will explore the importance of the audition in any phase of your life. We will learn how the audition in the theater is the most important aspect of an actor's job search. We will learn similarly that in the business world you are auditioning in some way or another every working day, whether it is for your next role, your next deal, or your next step up the ladder. We will learn that in everyday life, our relationships are, in many ways, an audition without end. Whether we are entering a new phase or ending an old one, each role requires an audition. Finally, we will explore the important elements in every audition and how we can use them to our advantage.*

DISCOVER

- How to prepare for an audition

- What transpires in an audition

- What makes for a successful audition

- How to relate to your audience: the producer and director

LET THE SHOW BEGIN

SETTING: Donald waits in the lobby for his audition. There are three other candidates awaiting auditions. He wonders if they are there for the same position. His hands are sticky and wet, his heart is beating faster than usual, and his mouth feels dry, like it's full of cotton. The auditioner approaches, and Donald has to wipe his hand on his pant leg before shaking hands.

This is a familiar scene in theater lobbies throughout the world. The part audition can be very stressful for most people. Since one of our greatest fears is *REJECTION* and one of our greatest needs is *ACCEPTANCE*, it is not surprising that auditions make people sweat.

Imagine auditioning in front of a director and a producer for a role in their play, knowing there will be 50 or 100 other aspiring actors competing for the same position. Imagine doing this every day, knowing how few plays there are in any given town and how few viable acting roles there are.

This is life. We audition constantly. The barista at Starbucks may already have a role that she auditioned for when she was hired, but the truth is, she is really auditioning every time a new customer steps up to her counter. Will they be pleased with the service? Will they be pleased with the product? Will they return next time they want a cup of coffee?

Before actor's agent and author Brian O'Neil became an agent, he worked as an actor. He was once told this by a famous casting director, "You have to bug these agents and casting directors. But bug them in a *good* way."

He told me later, "This seemed to me contradictory. Bug them in a *good* way? What did this mean? It haunted me! Later, as a talent agent, I would discover what it meant. And *still* I would have to bug people, bug them in a good way to audition my clients if I was to thrive as an agent. What words would open the door for the clients I represented? I was soon to learn. Much as agents must learn how and what to say to casting directors, directors, and producers on behalf of their clients, so must the actor learn to speak to agents, casting directors, directors, etc., on their own behalf. But actors don't know how best to communicate, because they are often unaware of specifically what those with whom they are communicating need."

O'Neil continued, "In this profession of acting, it is

especially difficult to feel a sense of control over one's career. The actor is constantly at the mercy of those who make decisions concerning his or her immediate and, sometimes, long-range fate. It is the talented and committed actors who know that acting is a business, and that persistence is a necessity, but who don't always know the inroads or the resources that can help to make persistence a more bearable burden."

KNOW THE NUMBERS

In training to be an actor, you learn that 55 percent of communication is physiology and 38 percent is tonality, but only 7 percent concerns the words you speak. Physiology is very important in how you bond with either an audience or a prospect. I don't speak *at* the audience or *at* a prospect. I don't talk *to* them. I speak *with* them. I connect with people as opposed to just communicating words.

Every audition ever conducted swings on this premise, whether you're auditioning for a play, a job, or a homecoming date.

Connecting at the visceral level in business is just like making that connection in the theater. On the stage, 55 percent of your communication is based on body language—how people walk, how they talk, how they dress, or how they slouch, like Willie Lowman. That posture is not offering people what they most want, which is hope. Body language in theater is how you project your character and reveal who he or she is. It's all about tonality: how loud you speak, or how softly you speak, or how slowly you speak, or how briefly you speak, or what accent you use. It's all about making an emotional connection.

Every audition puts you in front of a different audience and requires a different emotional connection. Tweaking the connection is a skill. But it begins by understanding the need to connect. Once you are aware of this, every audition takes on a different light; you are instantly more in tune.

> "If we listened to our intellect, no one would ever have a love affair."
>
> RAY BRADBURY

For the actor, this auditioning process goes all the way back to his or her efforts to secure a dramatic agent. It goes back to their first acting lessons. It goes all the way back to that first moment when you start to dream about being on stage.

AUTHENTICITY AND THE AUDITION

The truest thing I can tell is that every audition—from the theater to the boardroom—is all about being authentic. From a theater perspective, you have to trust the authenticity of the actor, whether he is playing Napoleon or Jesus Christ or Branch Rickey. You can't look at Harrison Ford in the Branch Rickey role and think: He's acting just like Indiana Jones. It

> "The hiring process is the casting in business. I wrote an article titled "The profit is in the hire," and one of my messages is, 'Hire slowly, fire quickly.' I also never say that we fire people. We return them to the labor market."
>
> BERNIE CRONIN

starts with Ford himself believing that he is Rickey. Without that, the message the screenwriter or playwright was trying to convey is lost on the audience. They leave with the feeling, "Well, that was okay"—not with, "Wow!"

We all remember the role of Jack Nicholson as the Marine Corps Colonel in *A Few Good Men*. As Eric Morris says, "Nicholson became that Marine Colonel. He didn't just play the role that was written for him. You have to develop that authenticity within you to get past pretending you are something you're really not."

CEOs may have many different roles, but CEOs must know when they walk in the door of that conference room or boardroom that they are "the man" or "the woman." You don't fake it, because people will sense a lack of authenticity, and then you're sunk. I think it's bullshit when I hear trainers tell their clients "you have to fake it to make it."

When you're a parent, you can't question yourself. You're a dad or a mom and you play the role with an air of total authenticity. Even when you're unsure of a decision or exactly what to do when your baby comes down with a cold, you press ahead. Authenticity doesn't mean you have all the answers. It means you're willing to admit when you're confused or need help.

> "How many times did Leno hear no before he heard yes? What did he do about this? He kept telling jokes."
>
> BERNIE CRONIN

CASTING IS KEY

Whether we're talking about the film industry or the business world, casting is critical. In 2013, after winning the Academy Award for best original screenplay for *Django Unchained*, writer Quentin Tarantino said, "You spend all this time writing the script and then you have one shot to cast the right people to pull it off. If you don't, you have an average movie, but if you do, you might have a great movie."

The same thing goes for hiring in the business world. Sometimes, your gut will tell you to hire the right person. And when it comes to casting, you have to trust those instincts. The best directors always do. They believe in themselves. They believe what they see during an audition and they believe what they sense.

"I hired him because I liked him" is not a good reason to hire someone. People will often hire people like themselves, as opposed to hiring someone who is different from them and looks at the world through a different lens. When Charlie Anderson came to work for us, I said, "Charlie, if you and I agree on everything, then one of us isn't necessary." I want some pushback. I don't need a "yes" man. You find these things out in the audition process. Jay Leno talks about going to audition for a part early in his career and seeing his resume in the waste can. Look at what Jay Leno is today—and where he would be if he had given up at that time. He auditioned, and he kept auditioning.

NOT EVERY AUDITION IS SCRIPTED

In my world, "no" means just one thing: "Never over." Keep going. I have a sign in my office that reads: "One more call." It used to read, "Shut off the coffee machine, paper in the fax machine." Now it's: "One more call."

Think about it. That's 220 dials a year to make before going home. Same thing with the theater, "Make one more audition."

Business is a never-ending chain of auditions.

In business, just as in acting, you need to learn to be present in the moment and to improvise constantly. The show goes on and the curtain goes up whether you're ready or not. You have to be able to adapt yourself to every situation, and to change in an instant.

Remember that as well prepared as you might be for your audition, the situation may very well call for improvisation on your part. You may have to improvise at some point in a job interview. You may have to improvise when you're talking to a pretty girl on the subway or talking to a group of potential donors to a charity event that's close to your heart.

Going into a business interview, for example, the reality may be totally different from what you expected. Maybe the central problem is that the owner's son is the manager, but you can't come out and say, "Your son is in the wrong place." I've seen many companies in which owners try to bring along a second or third generation who were probably a high C or a high S, but the job requires a D or I—a leader.

My job is to profile people, so that's what I do. I come back with a profile and say, "He's a nice guy, but probably not in the right role. He should be more in an operations role than a managerial one." I let them discover through my acting programs that Junior should be in another role and they should look for someone to fill his CEO role. I help people work not just *in* the business, but *on* the business.

I have a talk I give to top management. I say, "You are the best promoter your company will ever have ... and that's the bad news." It's your company, with your name on the front door. You built it, but how do you get someone else to come in and take it to the next level. Your biggest challenge is how do you replicate more of you to work *on* the business, not *in* the business."

In my own business, I work with a wonderful woman named Angel. When Angel auditioned for me, I knew she was right for the job because she asked the tough questions. She showed passion, persistence, and desire. She also demonstrated that she wanted to make money, and that was important to me. She was auditioning, but she was also holding her own audition.

On her first day, Angel accompanied me to a Keynote Address at a company that will remain nameless here. We were there to gauge their interest in our services. Angel jumped in with both feet. She sought out the owner in the room, got to know him, closed him, and delivered the business. I never dealt with him and didn't want to. She sold our services, and that was the ideal for me. It allowed me to keep working *on* the business, not *in* it.

Angel was poised and ready to improvise her role. In the theater, you typically play only one character in the production. In business, you have to be able to shift your characters and be a chameleon, depending on what is required. Same for the C-Suite or the factory floor. Sometimes you have to gauge your audience and improvise. Sometimes you have to sense the atmosphere in the room and slip into a different role.

That's what improv is all about. And improv is what wows your audience. Companies often like to get three bids for whatever project they are about to launch; three bids means two bids from your competitors. If you're just like the other two, then you're just another commodity—because they want to commoditize you

"How good are the seven ships in your fleet? Relationships, friendships, partnerships, leaderships, companionships, fellowships, and stewardships. Every one of these influences the quality of your life every day. Tend them well."
BERNIE CRONIN

and make the deal based on price alone. You don't want to be just another product or service. If you want only a commodity, shop for it online.

Like Jack Welch says, "If you don't have a competitive advantage, don't compete."

I always say, "A sale based on price has no loyalty attached to it."

You get a competitive edge by wowing them as you're going in the door—or at least that's when you want to make your strongest impression. And when you are auditioning in the theater, the very same thing holds true. You have to make an impression the moment you walk on the stage. You only have 60 seconds. If you don't wow them, you are just another walk-on actor. You need a walk-off homerun. It might not be scripted, but that's no excuse for failing the audition.

Auditions work both ways. One time, I followed up on an introduction to a manager of one of the largest telecom companies intent on selling him on our services. The guy had a degree in arrogance and started out by saying, "Oh, Bernie, are you on our approved vendor list?"

"I don't know," I said. Are you on my approved client list?"

Then I left. I fired him right then as a prospect, and it felt so good. He would have set me up to fail, so I responded to his audition by saying, "No thank you. Let someone else have him." I allowed him to audition, and he failed the audition in the most dramatic fashion. Bring on the next actor.

Auditioning is a double-edged sword. You don't want a person who will eventually set you up to fail, and you have to be aware of that possibility.

NEVER SEND A LETTER

Remember the movie *We Are Marshall*, about the Marshall football team after a plane crash robs them of almost their entire team?

There's a great scene where Matthew McConaughey, playing the coach, goes to the university president and says, "Mr. President, we are Marshall. We are going to field the football team. We're not going to win any games, but we only have three players left and the others didn't make the trip because they were injured. The rest are freshman."

In those days, freshman weren't eligible to play varsity football, so McConaughey goes on to say, "Mr. President, in order to field the football team, we're going to ask the NCAA for an exemption to allow freshmen to play."

The president looks over at him and says, "Coach, I'll take care of it. I'll send them a letter right away."

"Mr. President, can I ask you a question?" "Yeah."

"Are you married?"

"Yes. I've been married for 23 years."

"When you proposed to your wife, did you send her a letter?"

In the next scene, the president is walking out of the NCAA after a face-to-face meeting with them and getting the exemption the coach was lobbying for. Great stuff. Also a great message. Tear jerker. I watched it and was like, "Oh, my god. Great message and applicable in business and decision making."

In business, people will say, "Sure. Send me some literature." Don't do it!

A typical account representative puts a whole bunch of literature in an envelope, mails it out, and thinks that's business development. Instead of saying, "Wouldn't it make sense for us to meet?" he sends out the literature and goes to Hope Island. Rather than saying, "Specifically, what literature do you want? Why don't we make a phone appointment and I'll call you back for the next step?"

They don't take the next step.

THE POST-AUDITION PROCESS

The audition never really ends.

Whether it's the theater, your company, or your community, you want everyone to take ownership. The more ownership people feel, the more action they're willing to take. You want them to perform. We measure that in the theater based on applause and standing ovations.

In the business world, I recommend that managers do performance reviews of their people quarterly—behavior performance reviews, plus an annual evaluation. Do the quarterly reviews in March, June, September, and December. Use this to understand people's personal as well as professional goals. Not private goals, but personal goals like, "I want to buy a new home. I want to get married."

Look at their performance exactly as you would in the theater. Actors need to be passionate about their roles—they have to own their roles—or the audience will feel what's missing and the authenticity is lost. If the actor has passion, so does the audience. In business or the theater, passion is infectious.

In the audition process, your best weapon is your passion. Know when to wear it on your sleeve. Don't be put off. Don't think of rejection as a failure. Press on. Believe in yourself.

Remember the words of the great comedian, Jonathan Winters: "If your ship doesn't come in, swim out to meet it."

CURTAIN CALL

We are constantly auditioning. Auditioning is scary. It takes courage. Believe in yourself, and the fear will become your ally.

Fifty-five percent of communication is physiology and 38 percent is tonality, but only 7 percent concerns the words you speak.

Know the seven ships in your fleet—relationships, friendships, partnerships, leaderships, companionships, fellowships, and stewardships—and tend them well.

OUT OF THE BOX OFFICE (BERNIE'S PERSONAL CHALLENGE)

I challenge you to audition for a role you believe you could be cast for in a local upcoming play or repertory theater. Just show up for the audition and fill out the reasons you should be selected for the part. Even if you don't get called or choose not to audition, you'll get to see and speak with other folks auditioning for various roles and get an appreciation for the rejection and obstacles actors must confront every day in their chosen profession.

*"The profit is in the hire and yet most organizations
hire for skills and fire for attitude."*

BERNIE CRONIN

ACT 8

THE INTERVIEW

PLAYBILL

*In Act 8, The Interview, we will explore the similarities between
the interview process that occurs in workplace at all levels and how
it relates to the audition process in the theater. We will delve into the
intricacies of a truly effective interview and look at it from both the
interviewer's point of view, as well as that of the interviewee. We will
juxtapose the stage audition with the workplace interview and discuss how
the tricks of a successful audition can positively impact the rigors of the
interview process in the hard, cruel world. Finally, we will see how the
interview is, in essence, an audition and vice versa.*

DISCOVER

- Why the interview is given too much importance

- What a performer needs to do to prepare for an interview

- How both the interviewee and the interviewer need to prepare for their various performances

- What message you send your eagles when you hire turkeys

LET THE SHOW BEGIN

We begin by looking at what is essentially a man or woman's first interview performance: this being the actual interview for the position they are seeking. Here are the steps we need to consider:

- The candidate develops a resume outlining his or her education, work experiences, references, etc. (portfolio)

- The candidate responds to a want ad by submitting his/ her resume electronically, via fax, or by hand (call)

- An employer conducts an initial phone interview (pre-audition)

- An employer invites the candidate in for a personal interview (audition for the part)

- The candidate prepares for the interview by Googling the company, annual reports, mission statement, etc. (due diligence)

- The candidate prepares for the interview with haircut, manicure, best suit/dress, etc. (getting in character)

- The candidate shows up on time, prepared to show their talent (why they meet the job description) and why they should be offered a part in the play (full-blown audition)

I've written a complete guide on "HOW TO INTERVIEW (AUDITION) FOR ANY POSITION," and you'll find it on my website: www.berniecronin.com.

REHEARSAL

Every job interview starts with thoughtful, energetic rehearsals. Don't ever think of going into an interview without practicing your answers to every possible question. You have to know how to rehearse, however, and here are a few tips.

Monster.com contributing writer Caroline M. L. Potter is quick to tell us that there are a lot of necessary steps that precede the interview portion of your job search: writing a resume, networking, and compiling your references.

We all know about these, of course, and yet we somehow seem to think that *getting* the interview is the most important part of the process. The problem is that many of us fall apart during the *actual* interview. This is most often just lack of preparation.

As Potter tells us, instead of winging it or relying solely on your professional skill set, you should stage a rehearsal for your next job interview. This is not that difficult and can actually be fun. It is definitely advantageous.

Start by enlisting a family member, friend, or partner to play the role of the interviewer and ask that they stay in character from start to finish. We are, after all, in character here and playing the roles we've been given. Pretend you're on stage; pretend there is an Oscar on the line.

Step two: Become a set designer for a few minutes. Set up a space (set), such as a desk or table with all the fixings where you can create a suitable setting for your interview scene. The more authentic, the better.

Then use the following tips from corporate trainer Marlene Caroselli to make your interviews—both mock and real—successful:

- **Do Your Homework**—Learn all you can about the organization in advance. Share this information with your mock interviewer, perhaps in the form of crib notes.

- **Tune In**—Watch people being interviewed on television and make note of what works. Look for traits that make people likable and appear competent.

- **State the Un-Obvious**—This is one really intriguing statement about yourself. Something that differentiates you from the pack.

- **Think Outside the Box**—Creative visualization can go a long way. Like athletes, visualize the process in your mind and create the scene in advance.

- **Know Your Lines**—Actors do it, and you should too. Memorize a few short quotes and have them ready. They'll help you respond articulately to virtually any question.

- **Sum It Up**—The very first request an interviewer may make is, "Tell me about yourself." To answer this common interview question quickly and succinctly, have an elevator speech ready in case they want a brief overview of your career to date.

- **Be Tough on Yourself**—Research tough

interview questions and then provide them to your mock interviewer.

- **Capture It on Camera**—Have someone videotape your interview rehearsal. Then study your body language to see if it reveals confidence, poise, and enthusiasm.

- **Listen Up**—Close your eyes and listen to the recording of your replies to interview questions.

- **Stay Calm**—Work on being relaxed before your big meeting. When you get to the interview site and are waiting to be called in to the interview room, work on a brainteaser and focus on your breathing to relax.

Bernie's note: What works for the job interview works for the audition. Oh, and vice versa.

CORPORATE CULTURE

I define a business culture as "the sum of an organization's shared values, beliefs, and norms of behaviors." You better know these before you go into an interview.

In his memoir, *Who Says Elephants Can't Dance*, Lew Gerstner says, "I came to see in my days at IBM that culture isn't just one aspect of the game; it is the game. In the end, an organization is nothing more than the collective capacity of its people to create value." Going for an interview? Know the company culture, and make sure your interviewer knows you know.

In the horrific collapses of Worldcom, Enron, Health South, Global Crossing, Adelphia Cable, and Boca Raton-based conglomerate, Tyco, many wonderful and loyal people lost their jobs and pensions and the leaders ended up in prison. As the saying goes, "Fish rot from the head down."

One of my strategic partners is The Performance Institute, an affiliate of The Pacific Institute (TPI) in Seattle, Washington. TPI is a worldwide consulting firm specializing in identifying and helping to change cultures to drive growth. As my friend Mark Panciera, of TPI, says, "Culture trumps strategy every time." I wholeheartedly agree with that statement. My point? Be as familiar with a company as you can before stepping into an interview room.

There's a corollary between producing and directing a show and strategic planning for businesses. Corporations have strategic planning sessions annually where they plan out their strategy, just as a producer or a director have planning sessions for who they're going to cast in a play, what play they're putting on, where it's going to be held, and when they plan to roll it out to an audience. It's the same thing with top management. They should have a full and intimate grasp on their technicians, marketing, operations people, customer service people, you name it. In other words, their whole cast of characters. So when you go into an interview, make sure you express your appreciation for the entire organization and all they've accomplished. Talk big picture even as you're talking small details.

Producers and directors take the playwright's message and incorporate it into a theater scene. What scenes are we going to put in and what scenes are we going to leave out? The CEO does the same thing for his company and is often the best business developer the company will ever have. He should be, because he represents the company and is always out there growing his or her organization. The best of them don't micro-manage. How does this affect the interview process? The interviewer should represent the entire company, not just a slice of it.

If you micromanage in the theater, expect a degree of alienation between the actors and the director or producer. You won't have collaboration or alignment. The same goes in companies where you hear: "Marketing is not a department. It is part of business development." And marketing says, "Business Development sucks." Then the Business Development people say, "Marketing sucks because they've got lousy material." Everything is out of alignment. It happens all the time and the CEO's job is to keep those things in sync.

When you step into an interview, look for alignment in the different interviewers you'll face. If you get the feeling you're walking into a hornet's nest, you might want to ask yourself if that's how you want to spend your days.

When I used to mention "culture" to potential clients I'd hear responses like, "Culture is that touchy-feely, airy-fairy soft stuff my HR Director talks about. My job is to build shareholder value and put bucks on the bottom line." I don't hear that as much anymore.

I'm passionate about recognizing, defining, and building cultures from both top down and bottom up. Culture is the glue that holds organizations together under pressure—and the moral and ethical compass that guides employees.

When you walk into an interview, you should already have a feel for a company's culture. Do your research. Then don't be afraid to ask your interviewer to define the company's culture in two sentences. If he or she can't, then there could be trouble on the horizon.

When I visit a prospective client, my first question is, "How would you describe your culture in one word (and you can hyphenate it)?"

Sometimes, I hand out 3-by-5 cards for this exercise. I once visited the CEO, COO, and CSO running an organization

> "Integrity is what you do when nobody is looking."
> BERNIE CRONIN

197

and gave these cards to them and asked my question. The first person wrote down "Dysfunctional," the second, "Dysfunctional," and the third, "Good Old Boy Network." I left knowing they weren't good prospects for me, and three months later found out all three were gone. Another time, I was conducting management coaching for the seven regional managers for a large Boston-based company and conducted my survey of them on 3x5 cards (the respondent on the card is anonymous). When I presented them to the owner, he looked at me in disbelief and said, "Bernie, we have a problem here. If that's what my managers believe our culture is, what does the rest of my organization believe?"

Cultures built on greed, dishonesty, and arrogance brought down those giants like Worldcom, Enron, etc.

Academic studies, like those conducted by John Kotter and Jim Heskett at Harvard, have shown that positive corporate cultures yield higher profits and growth over time, compared to negative cultures. From 1979–1990 (including the stock market crash of 1988), Kotter and Heskett studied 32 US companies, including General Motors, Citicorp, General Electric, Hewlett- Packard, IBM, Sears, Xerox, and Eastman Kodak. In their book *Corporate Culture and Performance*, the authors reported that during that time the companies with constructive cultures far outperformed those with defensive cultures. The difference was dramatic:

	CONSTRUCTIVE	DEFENSIVE
Revenue	682 percent	166 percent
Stock Price	901 percent	74 percent
Net Income	756 percent	1 percent

As we say in golf: "The scorecard doesn't lie." Or, as I frequently tell my clients, "People can lie about numbers, but numbers can't lie about people."

Earlier in my career, I got to know my next-door neighbor, Thomas A. Murphy, Chairman of General Motors. I can tell you firsthand that he was a man with dignity and integrity. A former CPA, he was treasurer and a fellow board member of our little villa association of 16 homeowners, and he reported the financial results as if they were a presentation to the GM Board. I used to chuckle to myself and say, "What would my dad think if he knew I was a member of a board of directors with such a distinguished Irishman as Tom Murphy?"

I have a number of successful clients in South Florida, such as Banyan Air (voted number-one Fixed-Base Operator by the Pilots Association); Hill York Air Conditioning, a major air conditioning company; Atlantic Truck Center, a major truck and bus company; Port Consolidated, the largest fuel and lubricant distributor in Florida; Bennett Auto Supply, a major retail auto parts distributor; E-Builder, a construction

Software Developer; Best Roofing, one of the largest Commercial Roofing Companies; and the Keiser University family of colleges and universities.

The entrance sign on the office door of the Banyan Air owner, Don Campion, doesn't say President or Owner or CEO. It says "HEAD COACH." The employees are known as TEAMMATES, and Don even has a chaplain on board to cater to the family, spiritual, or financial needs of his teammates. He is very proud of the fact that his Parts Department Manager, a young female, started out as a phone receptionist and now manages a major department that supplies aircraft parts all over the United States and the Caribbean.

CEO's Founders Don Campion, Banyan Air; Gregg Wallick, Best Roofing; Dr. Arthur Keiser, Keiser University; Jon Antevy, E-Builder; and Vistage Chair, Jaynie Smith, Smart Advantage; are all members of different chapters of Vistage, formerly known as TEC, with chapters all over the United States. Don, Gregg, Dr. Keiser, Jon, Jaynie and their 15 chapters in Florida meet monthly for a full day of roundtable sharing strategies and best practices. I cannot say enough about Vistage and encourage all of my client company owners and CEOs to make the investment in time and money to further the growth of their enterprises. Vistage shows you how to create a successful business culture. I am proud to be an approved Vistage Speaker.

The culture of the world of theater, on the other hand, is

a place where players on stage have common goals: function as an interrelated team, give and receive feedback, and deliver a collective message to their audience.

Very few colleges and universities have made the effort to blend their drama and performing arts curriculums with that of the business schools on the same campus. Very few businesses, likewise, have made the effort to introduce performing arts into their corporate training programs. I applaud the efforts of those few around the world in Canada, England, and Denmark who formed a group called AACORN (Arts, Aesthetics, Creativity, and Organization Research Network). This informal global alliance of artists, academics, and practitioners are exploring the intersections between business and the arts.

PREPARE

We have talked about systems and methodology throughout this book. We have said that whether you're growing an organization or acting, you have to have one you can fall back on. Interviewing, believe it or not, is no different. First and foremost, design a system that allows you to (a) prepare and (b) deliver.

You want to prepare yourself physically, spiritually, mentally, and emotionally so you can deliver at the highest level.

From an acting point of view, I think in terms of preparing my instrument (that being my physical and mental self), by using Eric Morris's *In Shape*. To truly understand and define the character—who it is and what you want it to be— you study what that person was like, where they went to school, how they talk, who their family was; you get to know their religion, their politics, their business philosophy. In other words, you absorb everything you can possibly think about regarding that character and his or her role.

Your system is like a MapQuest or GPS, to use today's terminology. It is a defined approach that leads you to become "authentic" in your character. How do I "become" a serial killer, when I don't even like guns? How do I take on that role? How do I prepare for it and deliver it? How will I look and how will I walk? What message does the playwright want to convey through my character? These are the core questions in acting, regardless of the method one buys into.

I follow and suggest my Rule of 3 in Interviewing

1. 3 Candidates

2. 3 Interviews

3. 3 Interviewers

BERNIE CRONIN

This is what you need to know to be successful at your craft.

It's no different in business. You prepare yourself for each and every role by knowing that role inside and out.

If you're heading into an interview, know as much as you can about the role you're interviewing for. Understand as much about the job description as you can beforehand. Visualize yourself on the job, performing the tasks at hand. Visualize your interaction with your boss and your peers. How will your character act: strong or demure, assertive or patient, leading or following?

If the job entails growing revenue, your craft revolves around getting people to make a decision. Visualize this. Know your company's products and services before you go into an interview, just like the actor who is auditioning for a part should know the play inside and out—not just his or her part, but also the entire casts'.

FEEL THE EMOTION

In the theater, all systems are designed to make actors better at their craft than they were before they studied their chosen method. In business, all systems and processes should be designed to get a decision from the interviewee. And they should be designed for maximum emotional impact on the part of the interviewee.

You need to know this before you go into an interview (prepare). Do your due diligence and impress the hell out of the man or woman posing their questions to you (deliver). And remember this: while you're interviewing for a job or auditioning for a part because you need the work, the company has a need too; they need someone to fill a role in their operation, and that's why you're sitting in that interview room. That is their pain.

You want the potential client to *feel* that his or her company is not growing or is losing market share, that their prices are too low or their turnover too high, and because it is, you help them discover they need your services.

You say to them, "How does all this make you feel?" Ask it more than once.

If you ask them what they think, they'll say, "Well, I think everybody in our market is cutting prices. It's the economy."

If you ask them how they feel, they'll say, "This economy is killing me. It sucks."

But no matter what their response, you'll get a better sense of what they're actually going through and know that much more about their needs. You go into a sales interview with every intention of acting like an interviewer, and see your prospect as an interviewee. Most business developers have been trained, for the most part, to sell features and benefits. They like to say, "Our product is bigger, better, faster, smoother, and cheaper." That's not an interview, that's a speech.

I say, come at them from another direction, from the direction of emotion: "How are you going to feel if you decide to add our products to your line and your business grows by $2 million a month compared to what you are doing now?" Now that's an interview.

The right questions are: "How does that character make the audience feel? How does the audience feel about the character's plight? Do they identify with the tragedy that person is experiencing?"

If people can relate to the performance, they'll say, "I've been there," or "I'm glad I'm not there," and that's when you really connect with them on an emotional level.

> "The truth is that it's easier for women to use the word 'feel' than it is for men. Some men are too macho to do this—and they're missing out on a lot of connections. It took me a long time to learn to use the words 'emotion' or 'feel.'"
>
> BERNIE CRONIN

Think of it this way: You're always interviewing. And the more you're in charge in the interview, the more successful you'll be.

SEE, HEAR, TOUCH, NLP (NEUROLINGUISTIC PROGRAMMING)

The visual is what we see, the auditory is what we hear, and the kinesthetic is what we touch. Then we have taste and smell, which we don't communicate with, unless someone has bad breath or body odor.

The interview, just like the audition, can best be maximized by understanding how you take in information: Are you visual, auditory, or kinesthetic?

> "Good acting and good living all begin with good feeling. Take that into every interview you do."
> BERNIE CRONIN

I coach people to learn their own preferred mode of communication and this allows them to start to identify what other people's preferred modes are. If they're kinesthetic, they'll want to touch things. If they're visual, they'll want to see things. If they're auditory, they'll want to hear things. People who are more visual say, "I see what you mean."

The other day I heard a lady on a cell phone say, "I'll see you later."

I said to myself, "She's a visual."

An auditory might say, "I hear what you are saying. You're coming in loud and clear."

A kinesthetic may say, "Let me get my arms around this project. Let's connect on it."

I get certain clues from everyone. A good interviewer is going to be utilizing this methodology. If you're coming in for an interview, be aware of this. Know what the job entails when it comes to taking in information and imparting it.

I'll say to the people I'm coaching, "Who do you know who is highly visual? Who do you know who is highly auditory? Who do you know who is highly kinesthetic?" Think about it. Be aware of it. Make note of how you can use it to your advantage.

I teach them that their job is to identify these people in this way and then adapt themselves to them. Don't say to the other person, "I'm a visual and you're an auditory." Show them where they are out of alignment with their best mode of communication. This is a very important communication skill that can be used all across your life, including with your loved ones. Do you really understand how your wife or husband takes in information? If you want to connect with them more deeply, study these modes.

What does this have to do with the interview? Whether you're interviewing or being interviewed, you want an edge. Knowing how the person across from you communicates could be all the edge you need.

I heard a sociologist up in Boston say, "In the year 2018, 85 percent of the population in the United States will be computer literate. Only 15 percent will be people literate." This doesn't bode well for the interview process, so be both computer literate and people literate.

If you can hone your people skills, it can be the difference between failure and success, in life, in love, in the interview process. People communicate in a certain style, whether they know that or not. An actor must be able to articulate in the character's preferred mode of communication. The audience will connect with this even if they aren't aware of how that connection was made.

If you are going to be an effective performing artist, you must be good at appealing to all three modes of communication. If you have a speaking part, speak clearly so that the whole audience can hear you. If you're going to be conveying emotion or playing a sitting scene or a falling scene or a walking scene, you've got to be able to use your physicality to do all of these things. If you have a kinesthetic scene where you've got to hug someone, giving half a hug isn't going to work. Hug as if you really love this person.

NO-TIVATION

The biggest hang-up for most leaders is dealing with their internal fears and conflicts. With business people, it's fear of rejection or fear of failure. Failure is just another step in the process to success. I train my people in "no-tivation." I tell them that hearing "no" is good. If you get a lot of no's you'll eventually get a lot of yesses. I say to prospective clients who don't work out, "Thank you for telling me no."

Whether I'm auditioning for a play or prospecting for a new account, I know that I'm going to get a lot more no's than yesses. The more no's I get, the closer I am to my yes. Show me someone who's going to get a lot of no's and I'll show you someone who'll get a lot of yesses.

> ## "Attitudes are contagious. Is yours worth catching?"

If you get a "no" during your first interview and assume that's all you're going to hear, you're going to miss out on a good job down the road. We live in a world of rejection; make it work for you.

> ## "Your goals and your comfort ZONE will always be in conflict."
>
> ### BERNIE CRONIN

For other people, the core problem is—believe it or not—fear of success. Some are afraid of reaching a high level of success and sustaining it, so they stay in their comfort zone.

If you go into an interview, decide up front how important your comfort zone is to you. Do you really want this new part? Are you really excited by this new role? Can you handle a "no?" Or does it have to be a "Yes?" Your strength in an interview comes from being okay with a "no," and being willing to escape your comfort zone.

GO FOR NO.COM

My friends Richard and Andrea Felton in Orlando have developed a whole program including books, CD's and live programs featuring the value of NO. I recommend them strongly.

CURTAIN CALL

You want to prepare yourself physically, spiritually, mentally, and emotionally before going into an interview.

Whether you're interviewing or being interviewed, you want an edge. Knowing how the person across from you communicates could be all the edge you need.

Never wing an interview or rely solely on your professional skill set; instead, rehearse, rehearse, rehearse.

Never forget that an interviewer has a part to fill, just like a director has a role to fill, and that is their pain.

OUT OF THE BOX OFFICE
(BERNIE'S PERSONAL CHALLENGE)

CALMING TECHNIQUES

One of the best techniques to handle stress in any situation is through controlling and being aware of your *BREATHING*. Take deliberate, shallow breaths. Take air in through the nostrils and exhale, slowly and quietly, through your mouth. You should practice this technique before the job interview.

ACT 9

ACADEMY AWARDS

PLAYBILL

In Act 9, Academy Awards, we will explain how the concept of Academy Awards actually goes beyond the realm of film. We will explore how the best performances on the factory floor, the boardroom, in the home, and in the community have their own standards of award. We will delve into the fine balance between award and reward, how sometimes they go hand in hand, and how sometimes the two are completely separate. We will talk about compensation, a category of its own. We will explore the many forms of Academy Awards, from the paycheck to the pat on the back, from the applause to the wondrous feeling of doing what is right when no one is looking.

DISCOVER

- How not all great performances are rewarded

- Why compensation drives behavior

- How we are all stroke deprived

- How to recognize the behind-the-scenes performer

LET THE SHOW BEGIN

Rewards, recognition, compensation, happiness, self-actualization, peace of mind. People do what they are incentivized to do from birth to death: school grades, awards, degrees, salaries, bonuses, recognition, etc. Give people the wrong incentives and watch them perform the wrong behaviors.

You get whatever behaviors you reward. My belief is that rewarding seniority is dysfunctional. I often find that top performers have more room for growth than do bottom performers, and yet managers spend an inordinate amount of time trying to get bottom performers to perform better to justify why they hired these non-performers!

All good. And while we see these as positive vehicles of recognition, praise, and adulation, they are only one form of the many awards we seek in theater, business, and life. Let's see what else is out there.

I laugh every time I read about how a superstar baseball pitcher, who already earns a salary well into the $4–8 million a year range, can also earn a signing bonus, a bonus if he wins more than 20 games in a season, a bonus if he pitches more than a certain number of innings in a season, maybe even a bonus if he gets a base hit and who knows what else. Kind of ridiculous on the surface. However, maybe these major league baseball owners have the right idea, a way of keeping the pitcher motivated all season long, despite a high base salary, and awarding bonuses in direct relation to the exact behavior desired (and expected!).

Academy Awards are performance based. Whether it's the theater, business, or life, awards are the result of doing, of taking action, and of jumping into the parade feet first. Awards and risk go hand in hand. Almost everything that rates a reward has some risk involved in it. Some movies flop. Some businesses fail. Some relationships go south. Sometimes the best reward—the shiniest award—is the realization that you put yourself on the line.

AWARD HAS ITS MERIT

I preach that compensation drives behavior. But are we talking about dollar signs here or something deeper? Sure, we have to eat. We have to take care of our families, so a paycheck is important, especially in a capitalistic society. I have no problem with the executive who makes $10 million a year; I assume he's earned it. That's his reward. I've made good money in my life, and I'm happy about that. But I have also come to realize that it's the relationships I've cultivated over the years that are my real reward. My family. My friends. My colleagues. Personally I do have a problem with the disparity of compensation between many business positions and that of elementary and high school teachers whose responsibility to educate our youth knows little parallel.

Compensation is also about performance. It's okay to be proud of your performance and to have people shower you with applause. Heck yes. But it's the people who are backstage waiting to give you a hug and a pat on the back who last beyond that standing ovation. The people you work with, the friends and family who support you, the flowers sent by an unnamed admirer.

There is another point about compensation that fits under the category of well-deserved awards. Is the compensation fair? If a CEO feels she is being paid fairly, then that is an "award" in its own right. If the stagehand knows he's not being paid industry- standard wages, then the pride he might otherwise feel knowing his work contributed to a standing ovation for the performers is considerably diminished.

So let's not short-sell the Oscar for Best Compensation. Pay has its place. Pay makes up for a lot of shortcomings. Pay gives you leverage. Pay allows you certain freedoms. Pay is earned, yes, but it is also seen as an "award." And when the pay doesn't match the effort or the responsibility, it becomes an issue that other "awards" can't mitigate.

The theater and the workplace share another less than obvious connection with regard to our use of the word "awards." It's called the future; it's called your career path. When you do well, you get promoted. You work hard, you get rewarded. You perform, you get noticed. These are all rewards. A supporting role becomes a leading role. A supervisory position becomes a manager/leader's job.

THROW OUT THE TIME CLOCK

I always tell my teammates and clients "It's not how long you're here that counts; it's what you accomplish while you're here that counts."

One of my clients, Forte Interactive, a West Palm Beach, Florida tech company that specializes in web page development and management for non-profits adopted a *"results only"* work schedule that doesn't require employees to 'clock in' and allows them unlimited vacation time. The only requirement is that they complete the projects assigned to them.

It's an atypical approach to management, and even the biggest beneficiaries, employees who are encouraged to go home once their work is finished ---- can find it disconcerting.

One engineer said "as long as you've done your work and completed all your tasks, they push you to go home. Now

I can play with my kids."

Forte COO, Slade Sundar, said "the result is a happier and more productive work force. It stops a lot of the clock watching you find in larger organizations. We're getting better work. We're treating them like adults. We give them the goals and they deliver the results."

In an age of telecommuting, email, video conferencing, and skype, workplace experts long have predicted that work schedules will grow more flexible.

In concept I love the idea. Going back to my original quote "it doesn't matter where you work, when you work, or how long you work, as long as you get the work done."

But it's a scary concept for managers who want to squeeze as much productivity from employees as possible. Rob Anderson, a Founding Partner at Forte Interactive recalls that "launching the *'results only'* schedule was frightening". He wondered if anyone would show up for work. The fear is that people are going to take advantage of it."

"That makes hiring crucial –if workers can leave when they want to, employers must hire serious, motivated people."

And that's where I come in with the interviewing and profiling tools I provide my clients, including Forte.

And Forte Executives found the big challenge wasn't

getting workers to show up despite their freedom. It was getting them to go home. "We didn't know how to deal with the 'WORKAHOLICS' " said COO Slade Sundar.

A schedule free workplace doesn't work for everyone. Workers in health care and retail for instance, can't leave the hospital or store and labor laws require hourly wage earners to be paid by the hour.

However, I can see the arrangement making sense for professional organizations such as law firms, consulting companies, and architectural, accounting, engineering and technical firms. These organizations are typically staffed with driven professionals who often put in a few hours of work even while on vacation. And there is a strong financial motive for employers; by doing away with vacation time, they no longer carry unused vacation time on their balance sheets.

That huge financial liability goes away if employers say vacation is something employees can take whenever they feel the need.

For Forte Interactive, the schedule-free workplace is driven not by accounting concerns, but by a desire to hang onto hard to find technical employees.

MOVIES

We think of the Academy Awards with regard to the movies. In all, the Academy of Motion Picture Arts and

Sciences awards Oscars in the following 24 categories: Best Picture, Best Actor, Best Actress, Supporting Actor, Supporting Actress, Best Director, Foreign Language Film, Adapted Screenplay, Original Screenplay,

Animated Feature Film, Production Design, Cinematography, Sound Mixing, Sound Editing, Original Score, Costume, Documentary Feature, Documentary Short Subject, Film Editing, Makeup and Hairstyling, Animated Short Film, Live Action Short Film, and Visual Effects.

In terms of acting categories, there has been one constant in the selection process, from Mary Pickford in *Coquette* (1929) to Daniel Day-Lewis in *Lincoln* (2012), and that is that the academy favors chameleonic transformations over roles in which the actors seem to be playing versions of themselves. Though the latter performances tend to age better over time, these ultimate expressions of the self—e.g., Humphrey Bogart in *Casablanca*, Bette Davis in *All About Eve*, July Garland in *A Star Is Born*—invariably lose. I'm just as interested as you are in who gets snubbed. One of my favorite lists is the one of iconic performers who were *never* nominated for an Oscar for what we think of as iconic performances. These are my favorites:

- Sean Connery as James Bond

- Humphrey Bogart as Sam Spade

- Boris Karloff as Frankenstein

- Peter Sellers as Inspector Clouseau

- Anthony Perkins as Norman Bates

Are you kidding me? How did these guys get overlooked?

On the other hand, what I find most interesting is that these five wonderful actors may never have received "awards" that came in the shape of a statue, but their rewards were the more lasting kind: the recognition and acclaim that these roles brought them, the love and adulation of their fans, and the artistic praise of critics.

Yes, the statue is nice, but I think the emotional and psychological "Academy Awards" often have more deep-rooted meaning.

TELEVISION

In TV, we have the Emmy Awards. The Emmys are awarded in 28 categories by the Academy of Television Arts and Sciences. There are two separate annual ceremonies for Primetime Shows and Daytime Shows.

Here's another list of snubs for you, of some iconic performers who were nominated but *never won* for their iconic roles on TV:

- Jackie Gleason as Ralph Kramden

- Leonard Nimoy as Mr. Spock

- Larry Hagman as J.R. Ewing

- Bill Cosby as Dr. Cliff Huxtable

- Jerry Orbach as Lennie Briscoe

- Angela Lansbury as Jessica Fletcher

- Gary Shandling as Larry Sanders

Sure, I know these people would have liked to have heard the cheers as they walked up to the stage and hoisted their award, but the real reward here is creating characters who live in infamy. We will never forget Jackie Gleason sending Alice to the moon or Spock's pointed ears. That is its own special kind of "award."

THEATER

In theater, we have the Tony Awards, excellence in live performances personified.

MUSIC

In music, we have the Grammys, excellence we might not always agree with or understand, but recognition nonetheless.

GOLDEN GLOBE AWARDS

Finally, since 1943, the Hollywood Foreign Press Association, a tight-knit group of fewer than 90 journalists, awards 24 different categories in motion pictures, TV series, and movies.

MY 7 LIFE AWARDS—THE SEVEN SHIPS

So what about the schoolteacher or the factory worker? The stockbroker or the nurse? For me, the best awards that life has to offer are the relationships we make and cultivate. If you want to create a trophy case for the many roles you play in your daily life, I suggest seven places for what I call the seven ships:

- Relationships

- Partnerships

- Fellowships

- Friendships

- Stewardships

- Guardianships

- Companionships

Try finding seven more powerful, desirable awards.

When someone bestows their *friendship* on you, and you return the favor, what could be better? When you are granted entrance into a *fellowship* of like minds or like souls, it's because the members of the fellowship see you as special. A *partnership* can't exist without trust and respect, and there are no better gifts to share. *Stewardship* implies the belief that you are worthy of leadership, and that only comes from proving your worth day in and day out. *Guardianship* suggests truly that someone believes in your maturity and your responsibility, and imagine the power of such an award. *Companionship* is what we all want; someone who likes to be with us just because, and that's pretty special. And finally, *relationship*; this is what all of our success as human beings is based on. The strength of your relationships is the ultimate reward, the Academy Award of being a genuine human being.

It takes most of us a very long time to realize that the everyday Academy Awards aren't about things. A flat screen television is nice, but it's not an award. Watching a good movie with your wife and kids, now that's the reward.

Imagine an actor memorizing thousands of lines for the lead role in *Death of a Salesman*. Imagine him portraying a character that isn't all that likeable in the end. If it's a local theater in Palm Beach County where I live, the guy is probably getting paid peanuts. So why is he doing it? What's his award? Imagine the show ending and the crowd rising to their feet. Imagine them giving the actor a standing ovation. Need I say more?

COMMUNION

Communion is a crucial part of the Stanislavski System of acting. Interestingly, it is also one of its greatest rewards. Stanislavski taught, "The actor and the actress must bring their emotional lives to the parts they play. But they must always be at the service of the play and the character, and not mere personal indulgence."

When the actor actually reaches this pinnacle, it is, many of them have told me, worth all the sweat, blood, and tears that go into their chosen profession.

"The living exchange between the characters in a scene, the communion between them, is what rivets the audience's attention," Stanislavski preached. "The completeness of that communion helps each individual in the auditorium forget himself, and enter into the drama on stage. This is another kind of communion; the audience with the characters, with the story."

That's why we go to the theater. That communion that takes us far from our day-to-day lives allows us to escape all else, and be a part of a transformation. As a member of an audience, that is our award.

In the workplace, out there on the factory floor, it can be tough. A good leader knows this. He or she knows that the rewards can be few and far between. He or she knows how far a pat on the back and "job well done" can go. But the worker also has to understand the awards of his efforts. Knowing that you're supporting your family is as good an award as it gets, but we often forget that. Getting a hug from your wife when you walk in the door after a long day is an award that speaks volumes, and yet we often forget that too. Taking off a few minutes early so that we can watch our kid's soccer game is the kind of award we have to remember to give ourselves and give ourselves often.

Here's one for you. If you ask Stew Leonards, head of the legendary family-owned grocery store chain in Connecticut and New York of the same name, to describe what he sees as the awards of being president and CEO of his own company, he'll tell you it has to do with satisfying both the store's customers and its staff. As he puts it, "If you look after your staff, they will look after the customer, who will look after your profits." That's a helluva reward all right.

In the business world, we talk a lot about commissions, salaries, and bonuses. We talk a lot about numbers. And yes, the numbers are important. But I have always found the greatest reward in closing a new account is the realization that I have discovered a prospective client's need and offered a solution that lessened their negative feelings.

I never did find much reward or satisfaction in talking someone into something they don't need or want. That's not satisfying in the least. But sometimes a prospect doesn't know they need something until they talk to you, and you can show them the benefit of what you have to offer, a benefit that will make them appreciate your efforts, maybe a benefit that secures their loyalty and makes them a customer for life. Now that's an Academy Award in any profession.

WHAT'S YOUR ACADEMY AWARD?

I think every person needs to ask this question. What is the award that awaits you at the end of your efforts? Can you take a pen and paper and actually put it into writing?

It may be something as simple as knowing your family has food on the table every night. It may be knowing you've made one person's life a little easier because you happen to be in their world. It may be, as I said earlier, "doing the right thing when no one is looking." It may be looking in the mirror and knowing you are treating your employees the right way.

If it's that year-end bonus, well, that's okay.

If it's three weeks of vacation in Hawaii, that's okay, too.

Life is enough of a slugfest as it is; we need to know what we're working for; we need to know what we have and appreciate it.

I suggest making a list of the awards you're seeking. Write them down. Make them purposeful. Make them meaningful. Make them you.

CURTAIN CALL

Academy Awards are based on performance, and performance is about putting yourself on the line.

Try to make the Seven Ships a part of your everyday life and your rewards will be boundless.

Always do the right thing when no one is looking and your integrity will always be intact. Know the awards you're seeking. Put them down on paper. Believe you can reach them.

OUT OF THE BOX OFFICE
(BERNIE'S PERSONAL CHALLENGE)

I challenge you to write down your goals in the following manner. (See my Goal Card example below). Remember, Personal Goals always come before Professional Goals. The two keys are the time frame and the word WILL.

```
-------------------------------------------------------------

              GOAL SETTING
         94% OF WRITTEN GOALS ARE ACCOMPLISHED

   A PERSONAL GOAL IN_____ IS _____


   IN ORDER TO ACCOMPLISH THIS I WILL: _____


   A PROFESSIONAL GOAL IN_____ IS _____


   IN ORDER TO ACCOMPLISH THIS I WILL: _____


-------------------------------------------------------------
```

ENCORE

THE BLENDING OF THEATER, BUSINESS, AND LIFE

THE EXPERIENCE ECONOMY

In their book *The Experience Economy,* authors Joseph Pine and William Gilmore refer to people making buying decisions based on their personal experience, as opposed to, say, the features and benefits of products and services.

For example, they relate a coffee bean to first being a *commodity* that grows in Columbia or Brazil. Then they relate to buying the processed coffee bean in a supermarket and bringing it home to brew as a *good*. Next they relate to purchasing a brewed cup of coffee in a Dunkin Donuts, 7-11, or a convenience store as a *service*. Finally, they relate to my son Michael purchasing his coffee at a Starbucks as an *experience*. Starbucks is cool: dark wood, Wi-Fi, comfortable living room-like seating, and drink sizes called *grande*, etc. Howard Schultz, the founder of Starbucks, preaches to his employees: "We are not in the coffee business serving people; we are in the people business serving coffee."

Finally, Starbucks invests more money in training their people than in marketing their products and services, and all of their stores are company owned, as opposed to franchised.

The authors also talk about a Rainforest Café as providing okay food, but people going there for the rainforest *experience*.

DISNEY WORLD

Disney World is not in the theme-park business, or even the entertainment business; it is in show business.

Employees are called cast members, and they refer to being at work as *"being on stage."* The personnel department is called the *"Casting Center."* Cast members do not wear uniforms—they wear *costumes*, and they are not allowed to go onstage unless they are *"totally in character."*

Attendees at Disney World are not called customers or clients; they are called *guests*.

Disney World has a staff of 42,000, of whom 80 percent come in direct contact with their guests.

Like Starbucks, Disney World employees receive several days of intensive training so that every character knows that what he/she is doing is *"PUTTING ON A SHOW."* Even the cleaning people know that they are onstage, and Disney research shows that people with brooms are five times more likely to be asked questions than are people in Information Booths and those designated to answer questions, and, consequently, they are trained to perform that role. For example, if a guest asks a street sweeper, "Excuse me, how do I get to Animal Kingdom?" the sweeper responds, "See that small line forming over there at sign number two? The Animal Kingdom Bus boards guests every 10–12 minutes. The next bus is in eight minutes. There are two stops, the ride is 12 minutes long and Animal Kingdom is open until 9 p.m." Cast members are trained to speak in the positive as in, "The park is OPEN until 9 p.m," never, "The park closes at 9 p.m."

Mike Vance, the former president of Walt Disney University, tells the following story about his legendary boss, Walt Disney. A Disneyland Park attendant once spotted Mr. Disney down on his hands and knees. The attendant ran to his boss and said, "Oh, Mr. Disney, are you okay? Let me help you up!" Disney got up under his own power and dusted the knees of his pants. "Son, I'm fine," he said. "I'm just looking at my product from the perspective of my customer!"

Some Walt Disney beliefs and quotes are as follows:

"If you can dream it, you can do it. Always remember that the whole thing started with a mouse."

"We keep moving forward, opening new doors and doing new things; our curiosity keeps taking us down new paths."

"Do what you do so well that they will want to see it again and bring their friends."

MEMORIES

Alex Brennan-Martin of the Brennan family, who founded the famous Brennan's restaurant in New Orleans and Houston and the Commanders Palace in Las Vegas, speaks about memories in his co-authored book *The Simple Truth*.

In the book, he writes about one of his managers telling him, "The Waldrops kept talking about all the memories they have and about all their great nights at Brennan's of Houston."

Thereafter, Alex continued to ask customers how they saw the experience Brennan's delivered. "They all spoke of our service, food specialties we are known for, as well as our ambience and food reputation. But in addition, they all expressed the same sentiment; they wanted the occasion to be *memorable.*"

After opening Commanders Palace in Las Vegas, Alex held a staff meeting and told his team, "'Gang, we're all about memories, not food.' Their eyes lit up and smiles crossed their faces. The group picked up where I left off and began discussing the concept of memories. They had each heard similar terms from the customers but no one had put it as simply as I had. 'I agree we're about customer memories,' said one of the managers, 'but I think we should be about great customer memories. We want to be a great restaurant and a great place to work, so we need to create great memories to achieve our goals.'" The Mission then became "Creating Great Customer Memories."

HOTELS OF DISTINCTION

Hotelier Alan Tremain, in his book *Without Reservations*, details how he rose from the kitchen to beverage manager to assistant manager to manager of the Copley Plaza in Boston (now Fairmont Copley Plaza), to owner of the Chesterfield Hotel in Palm Beach (one of my favorite "thirst parlors"), to the founder of Hotels of Distinction. An Englishman, his career spanned the globe, from New Delhi; Hong Kong; New Zealand; Australia;and finally to Canada, where he managed the Empress Hotel in Victoria by the time he was 30.

He said, "There's a theatrical component to a good hotel— running one is like producing a play. The lobby and the public rooms are the stage sets and the staff are the actors. Most hotel people have a touch of the theater—the flash of the napkin as it's laid in your lap, for instance."

STEW LEONARDS

This legendary family-owned grocery-store chain in Connecticut and New York is acclaimed for satisfying both its customers and staff. The store makes its staff's needs a priority. Says President and CEO Stew Leonard, Jr., "If you look after your staff, they will look after the customer who will look after your profits."

THE BOTTOM LINE YACHT

My friend and client William E. Mahoney Jr., "Bill", owns a 90' plus yacht he bought from previous owner, Evil Kneivel, christened the "Bottom Line". Bill is the founder and owner of Mahoney & Associates, a Benefits Consulting firm who advises the likes of Citrix Systems, Royal Caribbean Cruise Lines, Jarden Corp., and New York Life.

Every Friday and Saturday, from September to May, the "Bottom Line" leaves its dockage from behind the Riverside Hotel, on fashionable Las Olas Boulevard in Fort Lauderdale, FL and cruises down the New River for dinner at the Chart House. It returns three hours later…you cannot pay anything. Everything is complimentary and a crew of 7+ provides drinks, appetizers and a view of some of the greatest homes on the river.

Bill Mahoney is the consummate connector as described in Malcolm Gladwell's great book *The Outliers*.

MY COACHING & ACTING STAGE

When my clients (guests) enter my theater, we do everything to make it a pleasant experience. If they are new to our theater, we have an Information Board at the entrance stating what the program is that day and, for first time attendees, welcome message with their name spelled correctly. Remember, everyone loves to see their "name in lights!"

We work on connecting with the guests' five senses (Sight, Sound, Taste, Smell, and Feeling). First you see the welcome sign and then, on entering, you see the continental breakfast. On the walls (Wall of Fame), you see testimonial letters from clients. Next, you hear the John Philip Sousa marching music. Third, you taste the fruit, juice, bagels, and coffee. Fourth, the room is sprayed before each performance and you smell the freshly brewed coffee. Finally, you are personally greeted, introduced to others, write your name on the chalkboard nameplate at your seat, and are made to feel at home. The sign on the doors to my office say "Backstage."

YOUR BUSINESS OR DEPARTMENT

Think about the experience your prospects, customers and clients have when they enter your office or place of business. What they *see* (testimonials, mission statement, pictures, periodicals, etc.); what they *hear* from the receptionist/ greeter, background music or noise; how they *feel*; what they *smell*; and what they **taste**.

Think about what your prospects, customers and clients hear when your people pick up the phone and greet them. Or, are you so blind to reality, or stepping over dollars to pick up dimes, that you have a lifeless, inhuman, automated telephone system that gives me 9 different alternatives and sends me to cyberspace if I don't know someone's extension. Get with it.

Two of the best and least used words in the English language are "THANK YOU!". I always answer my phone (even when my wife is calling) "Thank you for calling Bernie." I'm happy my phone rings because then I don't have to call someone else or a stranger with a Cold Call. And my phone message is the same: "Thank you for calling Bernie. Please leave a message and I'll call you back as soon as I am able." Short, sweet, courteous and to the point. I encourage all of my clients to use the same phone greeting: *"Thank you for calling ABC, this is Jeannie, how may I help you?"*

CREATIVE VISUALIZATION

In her book entitled *Creative Visualization*, author Shakti Gawain titles one chapter "YOUR LIFE IS YOUR WORK OF ART." She writes, "I like to think of myself as an artist, and my life is my greatest work of art. Every moment is a moment of creation, and each moment of creation contains infinite possibilities. I can do things the way I've always done them, or I can look at all the different alternatives, and try something new and different and potentially more rewarding. Every moment presents a new opportunity and a new decision."

"What a wonderful game we are playing, and what a magnificent art form."

CONCLUSIONS

So is business a *Broadway Show* or is acting a *Business Show*?

It's probably a question of semantics, but if you look at the desired results of both professions you'll find they lead their audience to an emotion and a decision based on the credibility of the performance.

Whether it's the teachings of Stanislavski, Meisner, Strasberg or Adler in theater, or Dale Carnegie, Brian Tracy or Tony Robbins in business, the goals are similar: to give the student a system or methodology for applying their craft in a professional and credible manner.

As a result of my experiences of over 40 years in management and business ownership positions, and as a student of acting, I've learned that both business and acting involve:

- Helping an audience discover an opening (curtain), a presentation (scenes), and a close (curtain). The audience interacts either consciously or subconsciously proving credibility.

- Teaching only from a position of having "been there, done it," and not academically from a textbook.

Finally, many corporation training departments, acting studios, and universities today are delivering a variety of programs, and the student must be very selective in what he or she wants to accomplish and learn. My biggest criticism of many training programs in both business and acting consists of what I call "EVENT TRAINING," a one-day, two-day or one-week event. I strongly believe individuals and companies are throwing millions of dollars away if there is not a reinforcement component to the programs.

My biggest criticism of the Training Departments of most of your Fortune 1000 companies is that they are made up of people who couldn't make it successfully in the field. So they became trainers, and one of the main reasons why many large companies (especially Financial Services) have such high and expensive sales position turnover.

Both business training and actor training are highly teacher dependent. Most teachers and trainers have the information, but not many are greatly gifted about communicating it. And, ultimately, business training and actor training are not about the information anyway. In both fields the trainer must be able to convey the passion, almost madness, about their respective craft.

What is it they say cynically in academia? "If you can't do it, teach it!"

PARALLELS OF THEATER AND BUSINESS

Building Relationships, as everyone knows, are the keys to business success. Now, what most people don't know is that it's not something on the prospect's desk, or his family or his tie or her dress; it's connecting at a visceral level. As I say, "People don't care what you know until they know that you care." Or, "You never have a second chance to make a first impression." Or, "First impressions are lasting impressions." Or, as Maya Angelou says, "People will forget what you said. People will forget what you did, but people will never forget how you made them feel."

My belief has always been that people do business with people; and people do business with people they believe and trust. I ran into a 40 ish year old guy in my pool and we were discussing what I do and what he does (insurance and financial services), and he said, "Business is different today. The 40-somethings shop on the Internet and buy on the Internet." I could not believe his comment and the only thing I said was, if you are a commodity, allow yourself to be commoditized, then why not buy on the Internet. He didn't get where I was going but I know where he's going ... Warren

Buffet said, "Price is what you pay, value is what you get," and Jack Welch, General Electric, said, " If you don't have a competitive advantage … don't compete." And, my friend Jaynie Smith, author of *Creating Competitive Advantage*, spells it out clearly in her must-read book.

Communion: This is a crucial part of Stanislavski's System. He taught, "The actor/actress must bring their emotional lives to the parts they play. But they must always be at the service of the play and the character, and not mere personal indulgence. The living exchange between the characters in a scene, the communion between them, is what rivets the audience's attention. The completeness of that communion helps each individual in the auditorium forget himself, and enter into the drama on stage. This is another kind of communion; the audience with the characters, with the story."

CURTAIN CALL
RIGHT BRAIN/LEFT BRAIN

We typically refer to refer to "Left Brain" individuals as linear, logical, by the numbers, etc. (scientists, business leaders, software engineers, professionals like lawyers and CPAs), and "Right Brain" individuals as creative, innovative and think outside the box (writers, actors, musicians, designers, inventors, teachers, and entertainers, etc.).

Daniel Pink wrote *A Whole New Mind,* a bestselling provocative book proclaiming that "Right-Brainers" will rule the future. Tom Peters called the book a "miracle." Pink dubbed this new world "the conceptual age," where "high touch" and "high concept" aptitudes are first among equals. "The future belongs to a different kind of person," Pink says, "designers, inventors, teachers, storytellers—creative and empathetic right-brain thinkers whose abilities mark the fault line between who gets ahead and who doesn't."

In a *Whole New Mind*, Pink claims we're living in a different era, a different age. An age in which those who "think different" will be valued more than ever. This new age encourages and embraces change and allows for the creative person to create artistic and emotional beauty while crafting a satisfying narrative. Although Pink does not single out the world of theater, one certainly can see how blending the world of theater and business is a natural extension. Writing, producing, directing, and acting to convey a message and transfer an emotion is certainly, according to my Right-Brain, a Right-Brain activity.

Bernie-isms

1. "Don't step over dollars to pick up dimes."

2. "Eighty percent of success is showing up."

3. Bernie's 10-20-30 PowerPoint rule:

    1. -No more than 10 slides

    2. -No more than 20 minutes

    3. -30 point font

4. "A goal should scare you a little and excite you a lot."

5. "If you're going to make a mistake, make it at full speed."

6. "Never is a long time."

7. "A goal without a plan is merely a dream."

8. "Most people only regret the things they didn't do."

9. "It's more expensive to hire the wrong person than miss the right person."

10. "What messages do you send your eagles when you hire turkeys?"

11. "A resume is a balance sheet without the liabilities."

12. "Taking care of you is taking care of business."

13. "We don't think ourselves into a new way of acting; we act ourselves into a new way of thinking."

14. "Make peace with your past so it won't spoil the present."

15. "No means we agree to disagree agreeably. Business is about NO!"

16. "There's always room for improvement. It's the largest room in the house."

17. "CEO means cut expenses often."

18. "Communication is sharing information. Connecting is sharing emotions."

19. "Money isn't everything; but it's right up there with oxygen."

20. "You were born an original, don't die a copy."

21. "Attitudes are contagious; is yours worth catching?"

22. "We don't train our people to hunt, we hire hunters."

23. "If you think training your people and having them leave is expensive, try not training them and having them stay."

24. "Don't take yourself so seriously. No one else does!"

25. "A sale based on price alone has no loyalty attached to it."

26. "It may be a small world but I wouldn't want to paint it."

27. "The greatest risk in life is never taking one."

28. "It's okay to have butterflies as long as they're flying in formation."

29. "DENIAL is not a river in Egypt!!!"

30. "Agreements prevent disagreements."

31. "You can't give away kindness, it's always returned."

32. "You can't buy a reputation, but you can sell one."

33. "Repetition is the mother of success."

34. "A goal without a plan is merely a dream."

35. "Ninety-four percent of all written goals are accomplished."

36. "Luck is where preparation and opportunity meet."

37. "There are always two sides on the streets of conflict. Look both ways."

38. "Four questions to always ask of yourself: 1.Why? 2. Why Not? 3. Why not me? and 4. Why not me now?

39. "Never let anyone out-prepare you."

40. "We need to first connect to ourselves before connecting to the internet."

41. "The more proactive you are, the less reactive you'll need to be."

42. "Learn from the past, live in the present, dream the future."

43. "It's a strong person who wants to hear what he/she doesn't want to hear."

44. "Experience is what you get when you didn't get what you wanted."

45. "Part-time efforts yield part-time results"

46. "After public speaking, negotiating may be the interpersonal activity most people fear most."

47. "If your thoughts were food—how healthy would you be?"

48. "We miss 100 percent of the deals we don't ask for."

49. "If you want to feel rich, just think of all the things you have that money can't buy."

50. "Why do they call it Life Insurance when you have to die to collect; why don't they call it Death Insurance?"

51. "How other people feel about me is none of my business."

52. "How come when I get up in the morning I can talk to God but I can't talk to you?"

53. "Life is not about finding yourself. Life is about creating yourself."

54. "Why work hard at being mediocre at something you don't enjoy?"

55. "While you're scalping me, why don't you give me a haircut?"

56. "This dog won't hunt."

57. "The last time anyone told me I looked hot, I was in a sauna."

58. "I call a bar a 'thirst parlor.'"

59. "It's not the size of the dog in the fight; it's the size of the fight in the dog."

60. "You don't have to be crazy to work here. I'll teach you."

61. "There's no traffic jam on the extra mile."

62. "The only 'Fast Buck' is in the Forest."

63. "Don't should on me!"

64. "The profit is in the hire."

65. "He's so cocky he sends congratulatory notes to his parents on his birthday."

66. "Notivation" ... NO is positive ... it is a decision."

67. "You can't spend overhead."

68. "You hire John Wayne on Friday and Woody Allen comes in on Monday."

69. "Don't confuse motion with action."

70. "You can make excuses and you can make money, but you can't do both."

71. "The call you make first is the call you want to make least."

72. "Characterological Deficiencies."

73. "Four out of three people have trouble with fractions."

74. "You don't stop laughing because you grow old. You grow old because you stop laughing."

75. "Growing old is mandatory; growing up is optional."

76. "Change is inevitable; growth is optional."

77. "You need a job to make a living; you need a purpose to make a life."

78. "You can't manage anything you can't measure."

79. "Power corrupts; PowerPoint corrupts absolutely."

80. "Not much sense growing old without getting crafty."

81. "Remember, when the Lord made time, he made a lot of it."

82. "DISCIPLINE: delaying gratification today at the expense of my long-term personal and professional goals."

83. "Excusitis and Victimitis."

84. "The education was good, but the tuition was high."

85. "Does he have 20 years' experience, or one year's experience 20 times?"

86. "Your goals and your 'comfort zone' will always be in conflict."

87. "Integrity is what you do when nobody's looking."

88. "That's not a lot of money ... you spill that much."

89. "It's only expensive if it doesn't work."

90. "'HOPE ISLAND' is for prisoners, actors, account managers, and business owners."

91. "Everybody knows 250 people."

92. "Qualify hard, close easy."

93. "Make a client; not a customer."

94. "You can overcome almost any obstacle in life except for two: Bad Heart and Bad Arithmetic"

95. "Miracles don't happen overnight; sometimes they take an entire year."

96. "He or she is 'FURNITURE.'"

97. "Either you own the business or the business owns you."

98. "We hire for skills and fire for attitude."

99. "Amateurs just SHOW-UP and THROW-UP."

100. "We don't fire ... we return them to the labor market."

101. "Most management problems are hiring problems."

102. "Leaders deal with vision; managers deal with complexity."

103. "SUCCESS is feeling fear, accepting it, and dealing with it."

104. "Work is when you are doing something and you'd rather be doing something else. It is "Livelihood" vs. "Lovelihood.""

105. "Work is something you do; not a place you go."

106. "Life is like toilet paper; when you get to the end it runs out fast."

107. "H A L T: Never make any decisions when you are Hungry, Angry, Lonely, or Tired."

108. "Keep the main thing the main thing."

109. "Keep your eyes on the prize."

110. "The bartender over-served me!"

111. "We are all descendants of revolutionaries and immigrants."

112. "Persistence requires multiple contacts."

113. "You can't send a Duck to Eagle school."

114. "Eagles never flock."

115. "I used to think a Hard Drive was driving in winter snow in New England!!"

116. "Turn NO GO into GO ON."

117. "I think he/she got their people skills online."

118. "I live at the corner of 'Hope' and 'Worry'."

119. "Don't rock the boat; capsize it."

120. "Fish rot from the head down."

121. "Prospects don't reject you; you reject your dreams."

122. "What's ahead of you depends on who's behind you."

123. "Why do you think Santa Claus is so jolly? ... Because he knows where all the naughty girls live."

124. DAILY MANTRA: "I expand in abundance, success, and love every day and inspire those around me to do the same."

125. "Exceptional people talk about ideas, average people talk about events, and small people talk about people."

126. "If Michelangelo was painting your ceiling would you tell him what shade of pink to use?"

127. "Beliefs drive thoughts; thoughts drive behaviors."

128. "If you're not supposed to drink and drive then why do bars have parking lots?"

129. "If there's a nip in the air I'd find it." (spoken with Irish brogue)

130. "People don't quit companies; they quit bosses."

131.   "We're all victims of other victims."

132.   "If we listened to our intellect no one would ever have a love affair."

133.   "Yes is the destiny. No is how you get there."

134.   "Never take a 'NO' from someone who can't say 'YES'."

135.   "Behaviors are beliefs turned into action."

136.   "The key to the bottom line is the top line: the numerator, not the denominator."

137.   "No one without a dream ever had a dream come true."

138.   "Be yourself; everyone else is taken."

139.   "Don't compare your life to others. You have no idea what their journey is all about."

140.   "Easy yesses produce little successes."

141.   "You never saw a hearse with a luggage rack or a funeral procession with a Brinks Truck."

142.   "I remember when a 'Gay Caballero' was a tough guy."

143.   "Quality doesn't cost; it pays!"

144.   "You can't learn navigation in the midst of a storm."

145.   "Happiness is no 'Tan Lines.'"

146.   "I refer to the morning newspaper as 'THE MORNING DISTURBER'."

147.   "There's always a lag time between the effort and the reward."

148.   "Passion is the process; goal is the outcome."

149. "If you think education is expensive, try ignorance"

150. "Wag more; Bark less"

151. "If you don't think there is a GOD ... try making a tree or a butterfly"

152. "Any day I'm vertical is a good day."

153. "All speaking is Public Speaking"

154. "He's tighter than a bark on a tree."

155. "If flying is so safe why do they call the airport the terminal?"

156. "Everyone talks about 'Good Fats' and 'Bad Fats' ... I like to think of myself as 'Good Fat'."

157. "If you and I agree on everything, then one of us isn't necessary."

158. "My most notable academic achievement was being elected president of my eighth grade class two years in a row."

159. "There are no insignificant people in any organization."

160. "Don't commit 'ASSUMICIDE'!"

161. "Success in business development requires 20 conversations per week with DECISION MAKERS."

162. "People only change based on self-interest."

163. "Change is your competitive advantage."

164. "There may be no 'I' in TEAM but there is in WIN!"

165. "Intentions are good but actions are lasting."

166. "You have to become comfortable with being uncomfortable."

167. "Vision is looking beyond the obvious. Success is doing something about it."

168. "It's not who you know that's important; it's who knows you."

169. "The difference between 'In-Laws' and 'Outlaws' is outlaws are wanted."

170. "I knew I could never become a lawyer because I've never met a bar yet that I could pass."

171. "The two most important days in your life are the day you were born, and the day you figure out why."

172. "In golf, a gimmee putt is an agreement between two guys who are both lousy putters."

173. "Your network is your NET WORTH!"

174. "Connectivity equals Productivity."

175. "I've learned so much from my mistakes,

176. I'm thinking of making a few more."

177. "Life is a theater, and whether you realize it or not, you are always performing."

178. "How can a war be 'CIVIL' when the definition of civil is courteous and polite?!!!"

179. "NO means 'Never Over.'"

180. "People never argue with their own data."

181. "Diagnose before you prescribe ... or it's malpractice."

182. "The biggest waste of time is a one-day Time Management Seminar."

183. "You can't manage time; you can only manage energy and behaviors."

184. "The average golfer walks 900 miles per year and drinks 22 gallons of booze, which is 41 miles per gallon."

185. "The biggest decision old people in Florida have to make is which directional signal to leave on while they're driving."

186. "Seventy-two percent of all statistics are made up."

187. "Fail fast, learn from it ... and move on."

188. "Customer Service is not a department ... it's an attitude."

189. "Logic makes us think; emotions make us act."

190. "Why do those who have nothing to do want to do it with me?"

191. "When the prospect is talking, he's buying."

192. "Today, overhead is on two feet."

193. "In business ... NO is a close!"

194. "Ireland is a shady place with sunny people."

195. "A partnership is a vessel that seldom completes its voyage."

196. "Golf spelled backwards is FLOG."

197. "Sigmund Freud is the guy who invented SEX."

198. "Your life will change over the next five years based on the books you read and the people you meet."

199. "Success is an inner concept and you carry it with you wherever you go."

200. "Always be a beginner, never an expert."

201. "If they're not laughing, they're not learning."

202. "Most people's dreams are to travel the world and write a book; why don't they?"

203. "Seventy-three percent of all statistics are made up!!!" (See Bernieism # 186)

204. "Habits die hard."

205. "I have a bad habit of liking bad habits."

206. "Why is it that everything I like isn't good for me?"

207. "My High School Yearbook was my Facebook!"

208. "Myspace was my part of the bedroom I shared with my brother."

209. "Online was where I waited for bleacher tickets to Fenway Park."

210. "Texting was a telegram from Western Union."

211. "So why are panties plural and bra singular?"

212. "Most meetings start at 9 am sharp..............and end at 10 am DULL."

213. "Do unto others as they would like done unto them."

214. "People can't drive you crazy if you don't give them the keys."

215. "If God wanted me to touch my toes he would have put them on my knees."

216. "Remember, you're not getting out of this life alive."

217. "Money is an exchange of knowledge and energy."

218. "Failure provides the seeds for success."

219. "Beliefs overcome fears."

220. "Find the PAIN or remain the same."

221. "Hold your tongue and say out loud... "DUMP TRUCK," "DUMP TRUCK," "DUMP TRUCK.""

222. "He's so cheap he buys his suits at Goodwill."

223. "Be wary of the 'WUDDLES' holding you back; wuddle they think, wuddle they say, wuddle they tell others, etc."

224. "Everyone's favorite radio station is WIIFM (what's in it for me)."

225. "So who's running the institution; the inmates or the warden?"

226. "Locks only keep honest people out!"

227. "Birthdays and golf have a lot in common—the higher the score, the more tempted we are to lie about it."

228. "Pay attention to who you pay attention to!"

229. "I call a telephone call center a 'cube farm'."

230. "Revelation becomes your 'REVOLUTION'."

231. "I think my 'GUARDIAN ANGEL' might be on vacation."

232. "NEGATIVITY can be self-sustaining within a group."

233. "The BOLD print 'giveth' and the *fine* print 'taketh away'."

234. "The truth will set you free; but first, it will piss you off."

235. "A procrastinator's work is never finished."

236. "Trade money for value...not time."

237. "I've reached the age where a 'Happy Hour' is a nap."

238. "FINISH STRONG!"

239. "It's hard to do well when you're hungry."

240. "I'm an introvert trapped in an extrovert's body."

241. "Perfection is a cruel tyrant."

242. "Done is better than perfect."

243. "If you're not laughing, you're not learning."

244. "The same days that I don't make people laugh, are the same days I don't sell anything either."

245. "There's only one God; stop applying for his position."

246. "The voice of fear will drown out all the other voices."

247. "All in...or 'GET OUT'."

248. "Procrastination is the 'Thief of Time'."

249. "If you're all wrapped up in yourself, you're probably over-dressed."

250. "Your destination will always out-distance you."

251. "If you get it for FREE; you probably paid too much."

252. "Change is your Competitive Advantage."

253. "Perform like a Champion...every day."

254. "Be someone...not something."

255. "A stranger is someone you feel strange with."

256. "Without a 'MISSION STATEMENT' you may get to the top of the ladder and then realize it was leaning against the wrong building."

257. "VISION is looking beyond the obvious. Success is doing something about it."

258. "TEAMWORK makes the dream work."

259. "Yes is the destination. NO is how you get there."

260. "Nothing great was ever accomplished by a realistic person."

261. "Compensation drives behavior."

262. "Rewarding seniority is dysfunctional."

263. "If love is all there is to know then all there is to know is LOVE."

264. "He who only hopes is HOPELESS."

265. "Culture trumps strategy...every time."

266. "Culture is to organizations the way personality is to people."

267. "Culture is what runs your company when you're not there."

268. "Change the way you view tomorrow and the way you view tomorrow will change."

269. "To keep a lamp burning we have to keep putting oil in it."

270. "Remember, all of us are descendants of immigrants and revolutionaries."

271. "Theater and entrepreneurship go hand-in-hand because they are both born in our right/creative brain."

272. "A coach is someone who can give correction without causing resentment."

273. "Failure is not fatal but failure to change may be."

274. "The best antiques are old friends."

275. "People who say it cannot be done should not interrupt those who are doing it."

276. "People can lie about numbers, but numbers can't lie about people."

277. "In order for you to be convincing; you must first be convinced."

278. "Replace 'IF ONLY' with........ 'NEXT TIME'!!!!!"

279. "The only purpose of your behaviors is to get results."

280. "Get up, dress up and show up."

281. "It's never too late to have a HAPPY CHILDHOOD."

282. "People skills are a science you study for a lifetime in which you can exhaust yourself but never your subject."

283. "Self Esteem is an objective and favorable impression of yourself which influences all of your experiences."

284. "Respect all....but fear none."

285. "If you don't like something change it; if you can't change it then change the way you think about it."

286. "People don't care what you know until they know that you care."

287. "Everything you have ever wanted in your life is always on the other side of FEAR."

288. "Success is loving yourself, loving what you do and loving why you do it."

289. "It's not who you are that's important; it's who you are becoming."

290. "If it doesn't challenge you, it won't change you."

291. "Our life is a reflection of what we believe we deserve."

292. "It's never too late to be what you might have been."

293. "Every golf shot makes somebody happy."

294. "The U.S. Constitution doesn't guarantee happiness, only the pursuit of it. You have to catch up to it."

295. "Coaching isn't an addition to a leader's job; it's an integral part of it."

296. "Mediocre companies have a transactional view *of* their clients while successful companies have a relationship *with* their clients."

297. "Money is only a problem until you've spent it."

298. "Visions must change as circumstances change."

299. "GO make a difference in the world.......because you CAN!"

300. "ROMEO'S are **R**etired **O**ld **M**en **E**ating **O**ut!!!"

301. "The most popular person in most NFL cities is the backup quarterback."

302. "Business executives are just kids in suits."

303. "H O M E stands for 'Here on Mother Earth'."

304. "Earth is a round planet and we are all connected somehow."

305. "Someday is not a day on the calendar."

306. "BUT & HOWEVER are 'eraser' words and everything spoken before them is meaningless."

307. "A man is clever by his answers and **wise** by his questions."

308. "To be a successful entrepreneur is to be a true **'CONTRARIAN'.** "

309. "Failing doesn't define you; it helps you define yourself."

310. "Quick deciding is more important than quick thinking."

311. "The things that got me to this level may be the same things holding me back from getting to the next level."

312. "You are never your best.....YET."

313. "On your next trip to New York City tell the cab driver if you like the ride you'll pay him."

314. "I have a rich 'fantasy life'."

315. "Build your work style around your lifestyle."

316. "The good can keep you from the 'GREAT'."

317. "Find people who will challenge you, believe in you and inspire you to improve."

318. "The more I prepare, the more I prosper."

319. "People don't buy what you do……they buy WHY you do it."

320. "Poor people have large TVs. Rich people have large libraries."

321. "Who you know gets you in the door. What you know keeps you there."

322. "Hard work beats talent when talent doesn't work hard."

323. "I like the smell of a 'paid car' over a new car….any day."

324. "If they perceive we're equal they'll decide on price."

325. "Remember, everyone you meet is fighting a hard battle."

326. "Success is 10% inspiration, and 90% knowing who to ask!!"

327. "Have a **G-MINUTE** every day; Be grateful for your family, health, friends, education, respect, accomplishments and being able to express gratitude to others."

328. "If you don't have an assistant; then **you** are the assistant."

329. "When opportunity knocks you can't say "Come Back Later.""

330. "A Big Shot is a 'little shot' who kept shooting."

331. "My 3 most important events to focus on are: 1. Where have I been? 2. Where am I now? and 3. Where am I going?"

332. "Energy is the fundamental engine of high performance."

333. "Ideas make you feel good; actions make you money."

334. "FEAR stands for 'False Expectancies Appearing Real'."

335. "FEAR represents 'Forget Everything About Rejection'!"

336. "Support, Encourage and Compliment your relationships."

337. "I don't get paid by the hour, I get paid for what I bring to the hour."

338. "Listen to understand....not to respond."

339. "It's all about what's inside."

340. "What one step can you take toward your dream today?"

341. "Forget Plan B.........stick to PLAN A!"

342. "Who can you make laugh or feel loved today?"

343. "Your LIFE is your 'work of art'."

344. "Fear is a wonderful servant, put a terrible master."

345. "If you got it for nothing, you probably paid too much."

346. "Who will you inspire today?"

347. "What one step can you take toward your dream today?"

348. "Who can you make laugh or feel loved today?"

349. "You cannot go back and make a new beginning, but today you can make a new ending."

350. "What do we do if Google doesn't know?"

351. "The difference between success and failure is not chance but choice."

352. "The hardest words to listen to are the ones we need to hear the most."

353. "Is he the Decision Maker or the Decision Faker?"

354. "Life is a theater and whether you realize it or not, you are always performing."

355. "Beware of the gravitational pull of the status quo!!!"

356. "Focus on 'mindshare', NOT 'market share'."

357. "Quality doesn't cost, it pays."

358. "Fear of success sabotages your every effort."

359. "Fear of loneliness pushes you into unhealthy relationships."

360. "Fear of looking foolish keeps you from speaking up."

361. "I help make my clients' dreams come true....they don't need Mickey Mouse."

362. "Behind every rolling ball comes a running child."

363. "On my death bed I want my hair to be messed, be out of breath and not throwing up!!!"

364. "Every night I turn my worries over to God. He's going to be up all night anyway."

365. "Success is the ability to accept fear, feel it and conquer it."

RECOMMENDED READING/

LISTENING/STUDY

BUSINESS

Good to Great by Jim Collins

The E-Myth Revisited by Michael Gerber

EXPERIENCE

The Experience Economy by Joseph Pine and William Gilmore

In Search of Excellence by Tom Peters

Reengineering the Corporation by Michael Hammer and James Champy

EMOTIONS

Emotional Intelligence by Daniel Goleman

FEAR

Feel the Fear and Do It Anyway by Susan Jeffers

GOAL SETTING

Think and Grow Rich by Napoleon Hill

LEADERSHIP

On Becoming a Leader by Warren Bennis

PUBLIC SPEAKING

The Persuasive Edge by Dr. Myles Martel

SALES

How to Win Friends and Influence People by Dale Carnegie

SELF TALK

What You Say When You Talk to Yourself by Dr. Shad Helmsetter

THEATER

No Acting Please by Eric Morris

Acting, Imaging and the Unconscious by Eric Morris

Acting as a Business by Brian O'Neil

Improv: Improvisation and the Theater by Keith Johnstone

Improvisation for the Theater by Viola Spolin

Creating Conversations: Improvisation in Everyday Discourse by R. Keith Sawyer

Improv Wisdom; Don't Prepare, Just Show Up by Patricia Ryan Madson

JOHN WAYNE: The Life and Legend by Scott Eyman

The Great Acting Teachers...and Their Methods by Richard Bristoff

The Art of the Actor by Joan Benedetti

Your Life As A Movie by Francesca Banting

VISUALIZATION

Creative Visualization by Shakti Gawain

NATIONAL ACTING PROGRAMS

IN FLORIDA:

Burt Reynolds Institute for Film and Theater
P.O. Box 264
Jupiter, FL 33468

The Actors Workshop Of South Florida
P.O. Box 5134
Deerfield Beach, FL 33442

NATIONALLY:

Actors Studio/New School New School for Social
Research Actors Studio M.F.A. Program
68 5th Avenue,
New York, NY

1001 American Conservatory Theater
30 Grant Street
San Francisco, CA 94108

Academy of Art University
79 New Montgomery Street
San Francisco, CA 94105

American Repertory Theater
Institute for Advanced Theater Training
at Harvard University Loeb Drama Center
64 Brattle Street
Cambridge, MA 02138

California Institute for the Arts School of Theater
2470 McBean Parkway
Valencia, CA 91355

Columbia University School of the Arts
405 Dodge Hall
New York, NY 10027

Herbert Berghof Studios 120 Bank Street
New York, NY 10014 The Juilliard School
60 Lincoln Center Plaza
New York, NY 10023

The New Actors Workshop
259 West 30th Street
New York, NY 10001

New York Film Academy www.nyfa.edu

New York University Tisch School of the Arts
100 Washington Square
East New York, NY 10003

Northwestern University Department of Theater
1979 Sheridan Road
Evanston, IL 60208

Stella Adler Conservatory of Acting
419 Lafayette Street
New York, NY 10003

University of Illinois Urbana-Champaign
Department of Theater
Krannert Center for The performing Arts
Urbana, IL 61801

University of Washington School of Drama
Seattle, WA 98195

University of Wisconsin at Milwaukee Professional
Theater Training Program
P.O. Box
413 Milwaukee, WI 53201

Yale University School of Drama
Box 208325
New Haven, CT 06520

National Association of Schools of Theater (NAST)
*182 members

International Drama and Theater Education
Association
(IDEA) 90 Countries

Toastmasters International
Rancho Santa Margarita, CA

BERNIE'S ACTING PROGRAMS & TESTIMONIALS

"WEEKEND AT BERNIE'S"

OVERVIEW

Our acting and performance improv workshops conducted by Bernie Cronin with Professional Actors and Acting Trainers encourage students to discover and nurture their creative potential.

The workshops help students build self-confidence and develop communication skills as well as give them the opportunity to learn about the skills necessary for professional theater.

Our workshops include an Introduction to Theater basics, including theater games, improvisation, movement, vocal and physical expression, character preparation, scene study and storytelling, as well as writing and public speaking.

One-Day Workshops are conducted quarterly in South

Florida and can be customized and delivered in either a One-Day or Two-Day Format anywhere in the world.

Our workshops are directed, produced, and facilitated by Frank Licari, an original Blue Man Group actor and owner of Quite Frankly Productions in Palm Beach Gardens, Florida. He has been a professional actor for over 20 years and has a Certificate in Theater from The American Musical & Dramatic Academy in New York. He has performed in over 55 stage plays in New York, Boston, Chicago, Toronto and Florida. His TV credits include *Law & Order* and CBS's *Dellaventura* starring Danny Aiello.

PRAISE FOR BERNIE'S ACTING WORKSHOPS

Here's what they said about our One-Day and Two-Day Acting Workshops:

"A truly great experience—I had never had speech training before and I hope this will bring me up to a higher level in my career."
—Lesley Frohman, Sherlock Finders

"After this Bootcamp, I will transform and evolve to become the one I truly am. It's my responsibility to accomplish this."
—Alex Funkhouser, Sherlock Finders

"Excellent program to improve presence when speaking in front of people. It should be a requisite for a number of industries for Leadership Training."
–*Keith Duffy, Consultant*

"Your instructors were some of the best I have ever had the pleasure of training with."
–*Rick Zobel, Port Consolidated*

"Everyone bared their soul and this program helped me become a leader."
–*John Moore, Sandler Trainer, PA*

"Fantastic, excellent."
–*Joe Ippolito, Sandler Trainer, MA*

"The program makes you think; clean out some old tapes mentally and replace them   with new, more positive ideas."
–*Janet Hoose, PortConsolidated*

"Hypnotically positive! Anything is possible!!"
–*Steve Neil, IMI Norgren*

"Probably without a doubt the best workshop I've attended."
–*Kevin Barnabe, SECNAP*

"It was one of the most effective programs for my life experience that I have experienced in my adult life and will benefit professionally, in my family and community."
–*Monte Lambert, Forte Interactive*

"Eye-opening, better than expected. Recommended to anyone."
–*Rob Anderson, Forte Interactive*

"Everyone I know could benefit from taking this program greatly."
–*Gene Van Praag, Ernst Van Praag, Inc.*

"To be able to be 'present' is an experience where you want to live continuously. This program helped me by making me aware of the present while public speaking."
–*Miguel Molina, Quaxar*

"Extremely helpful, fun, interesting, and enjoyable. Pace was excellent, the days flew by."
–*Jim Morelli, IMI Norgren, Hartford, CT*

"Great adventure in discovering one's strengths and ways to improve one's weaknesses."
–*Alex Funkhouser, Sherlock Finders*

For more information or to book a program, call Bernie at

(954) 295-9202

or email him at

bernie@berniecronin.com.

"COMING ATTRACTIONS"

Bernie's Speaking Topics

HAVE BERNIE CRONIN SPEAK AT YOUR NEXT EVENT!

Bernie Cronin is available for keynote presentations and seminars. As a National Speakers Association speaker, Bernie is thought provoking, passionate, entertaining, and audience focused. His audiences come away with positive action-packed ideas and strategies.

His engaging and interactive sessions range from a keynote to a one to five day workshop. Whatever the length, his audiences are challenged to get out of their "Comfort Zones" and reach out to embrace change and innovation.

He has a menu of topics involving change, behavioral management, personal growth, and how to reach one's true potential.

For more information call (954) 295-9202 or go to:

www.berniecronin.com

or e-mail Bernie at

bernie@berniecronin.com.

Keynote Speaking and Lecture Topics

By Bernie Cronin

ONE HOUR TO EIGHT HOURS

1. "SHOWTIME" … blending the worlds of theater, business and life for greatness

    - The similarities of theater, business and life

    - Shakespeare: "All the world's a stage and all the men and women are merely players"

    - Storytelling

    - A Hollywood Celebrity, a New York CEO, a Chicago Salesman, a Boise Schoolteacher, a Boston Student … what do they all have in Common?

2. CHANGE IS GOOD … YOU GO FIRST

    - Fear of what might happen

    - Change agents

    - Lifetime reach-backs

    - Supports you need

3. HOW TO BREAK OUT OF YOUR COMFORT ZONE & REACH YOUR TRUE POTENTIAL

- Somebodies > anybodies > nobodies

- If you are what you do; then when you don't you aren't

- The Upside Down World

- Discover why your Goals and your Comfort Zone will always be in conflict

4. HOW GOOD ARE THE SHIPS IN YOUR FLEET?

- Companionships

- Relationships

- Friendships

- Fellowships

- Kinships

- Partnerships

- Hardships

"If your ship doesn't come in, swim out to meet it"
– Jonathan Winters

5. GOAL-SETTING: Personal, Professional, Career Planning

- 94 percent of all written goals are accomplished

- 3 percent of the population have goals; and everyone else works for them

- A Goal without a plan is merely a dream

- The S-M-A-R-T Model for setting realistic goals

6. PRESENTING YOURSELF WITH POWER

- How Do You Know How To Present For Their Reasons; Not Yours?

- People Make Decisions For Their Reasons; Not Yours.

- RULE: Tell them what you're going to tell them; Tell them; Tell them what you told them

- Know what you want your audience to act upon

7. HOW TO IMPROVE YOUR PERFORMANCE 50 PERCENT THROUGH POWER LISTENING & QUESTIONING

- Active Listening

- Asking Questions

- Applying the 30/70 Rule in Communicating

- 7 Power Words

8. WIN-WIN NEGOTIATING

- B A T N A (Best alternative to a negotiated agreement)

- Negotiating vs. Compromising

- The "Flinch Negotiating Gambit"

- 7 Tips from The Harvard Negotiation Institute

9. TEAM BUILDING

- How Well Are Team Goals Aligned With Organizational Goals?

- How Do You Differentiate "Lone Rangers" from "Team Players?"

- What Role Does HR Play In Team Building?

- How well do you know your organization's Team Culture

10. ORGANIZATIONAL LEADERSHIP

- Leaders Deal With Vision, Managers Deal With Complexity!

- What Message Do You Send Your Eagles When You Hire Turkeys?

- How Well Do You Know Where You're Going and Who Will Go With You?

- Organizations change; people go through transition

11. SUPERIOR CUSTOMER LOYALTY

- Superior Customer/Client Service is an Organizational Responsibility

- Dissatisfied Customers Talk More About Your Business Than Satisfied Customers.

- How Do You Make Dealing With Your Organization an "EXPERIENCE" versus an Event?

- Learn how to create an "EXPERIENCE" for the People you inter-connect with

12. CONFLICT RESOLUTION

- Conflict among the Team is Beneficial, if it is identified and managed

- The Best People to Resolve the Conflict Are Those in the Conflict

- Understanding the Difference between Overt and Covert Conflict

- How to Have a Conflict Management Process in Place

13. STRATEGIC PLANNING

- How Well Does Your Mission Align with Your Vision?

- How Well Do You Know Who To Involve In Your Planning?

- How Well Do Your Stakeholders buy in to where you're going?

- "Culture trumps strategy every time"

14. HIRING and MANAGING TOP PERFORMERS

- How Do You Know Which Profiling Tools to Utilize in Hiring?

- 92 percent of People Are Hired Because Of How Well They Interview

- How Good Are Your People at Interviewing?

- How Do You Train, Measure Behaviors and Compensate?

15. TRADE SHOWS, CONFERENCE, CONVENTIONS, EXPOS

- The Five Hints for an Effective Trade Show Performance

- The Seven Tips for Effective Trade Show Planning

- The Nine Neglects at Trade Shows, etc.

- The 15 Objectives at Trade Shows, etc.

"It's never too late to be what you might have been"

GEORGE ELIOT

"Imagine how many epic individuals there would be in this world if only we had scripted and produced our lives like a movie studio."

**FRANCESCA BANTING,
"YOUR LIFE AS A MOVIE"**

EPILOGUE

Karl Pillemer, a Professor at Cornell University, interviewed more than a thousand older Americans from different economic, educational and occupational backgrounds and asked them to share the most valuable lessons they learned.

Overwhelmingly, the focus wasn't on what they did, <u>but what they didn't do.</u>

Of a thousand people in the later stages of life, what

dominated their advice on the lessons of life was <u>regret.</u>

One man in his eighties was asked:

"If you could come back and live the life of anyone, who would you want to come back as?

<u>His answer;</u>

"I would want to come back as the man I could have been but never was."

He went on to say,

"This time I would act with more courage.

I wouldn't allow my fears to turn me away from opportunities I didn't take.

I'd risk more. I'd take the chances I wish I had.

I'd allow myself to fail more, love more and laugh more.

This time I'd be sure to live more."

WOW!!! Don't wait until you're eighty and filled with regret

Be the person you could have been….**NOW!!**

ACTION

Grab a pen and a piece of paper.

Now imagine that you are the hero or heroine of the movie that is your life.

Would your hero or heroine be.....?

Brave?

Passionate?

The one that shines the brightest in a room of people?

The leader of the pack?

A creator of great ideas?

The most loving parent a child can conceive of?

A compassionate human being?

A bold risk taker?

Whatever you desire for your hero, write it down.

Then, start becoming that person, NOW!

LIGHTS, CAMERA, ACTION!

BERNIE'S LEGACY

The next book I hope to write might be titled:

"YOU DON'T GO TO COLLEGE TO GET A JOB"

My message will be *"You Go to College to learn how to learn!"*

I advise all of my grandchildren and young people that when they attend college they take 3 Drama Classes. If the college has a School of Drama all the better. If not find a local Acting Group (see Addendum C).

Finally, after graduating from College, I advise they sign up with a Local Toastmasters International Chapter to learn and perfect the Art of Presenting and Public Speaking.

It helped me tremendously in learning how to present and overcome one of the greatest fears….

PUBLIC SPEAKING !!!

ABOUT THE AUTHOR

BERNARD M. CRONIN, CMS

Bernie Cronin, President and Founder of Bernie Cronin International brings over 30 years of direct sales and sales management experience to the firm's clients. Bernie's real-life, problem-solving skills combined with his communications expertise enables him to provide a unique, thorough and hands-on approach to the challenges of leadership, management, client development, and hiring that his audiences are facing.

During his career in investment banking, import-export, training, and sales and communications consulting, Mr. Cronin has worked with a variety of companies and industries. The goals were to increase profitable revenue and client development through the implementation of a philosophy of personal and organizational growth through gradual, incremental and behavioral changes.

He and his associates also provide in-house, customized, Corporate Consulting Services to assist organizations in achieving their revenue and leadership objectives. This is accomplished through consistent, customized reinforcement coaching.

His organizational engagements typically involve Four Steps: (1) Corporate and individual Assessments utilizing Business Development Process Audits and Team Assessments (2) Impact Coaching which can consist of Eight 2 Hour Sessions or 2 Day Bootcamps (3) Reinforcement Coaching (weekly, monthly, semi-monthly or quarterly) and (4) Customized Management & Leadership Coaching.

He is a graduate of the University of Connecticut School of Business and attended Harvard University's Extension School, where he completed graduate courses in Microcomputers & Information Technologies, Business & Organizational Communications and The Harvard Negotiation Institute.

Memberships include South FL UCONN Alumni Association, Congressional Country Club, Delray Dunes Golf & Country Club, National Speakers Association, University of Limerick Florida Advisory Board, The Ireland-U.S. Council and The Sheridan House Family Ministry.

Some of the organizations he has provided coaching, consulting and speaking services to are:

- General Dynamics
- Vistage International
- Construction Executives Assoc.
- Minolta Business Systems
- Boston Herald
- Clear Channel Communications

- Greater Ft. Lauderdale Realtors

- New York Life Insurance Co.

- UBS Financial Services

- Financial Executives Networking

- Siemens Medical

- Golf Course Superintendents Assoc.

- Parker Hannifin

- Xerox

- Merrill Lynch